Hacked Off

Hacked Off

One Man's All-or-Nothing Bid to
Crack the Secret of Golf

Tony Lawrence

For Jan, for everything

First published in Great Britain
2009 by Aurum Press Ltd
7 Greenland Street
London NW1 0ND
www.aurumpress.co.uk

A catalogue record for this book is available from the British Library.

ISBN 978 1 84513 460 0

1 3 5 7 9 10 8 6 4 2

2009 2011 2013 2012 2010

Typeset in Filosofia by SX Composing DTP, Essex
Printed by MPG Books, Bodmin, Cornwall

Contents

ONE
BEYOND A JOKE

'He enjoys that perfect peace, that peace beyond all understanding, which comes at its maximum only to the man who has given up golf'

— P.G. Wodehouse

1:54 p.m., 29 July 2004: I had visualised the shot to perfection. There was no need for power from the 7th tee at Burhill's Old Course. Just a controlled three-wood, played with a hint of draw over a cluster of pines, landing on the near side of the fairway to leave a mid-iron to the green.

I reopened my eyes, breathed deeply and lined up, rehearsing the crossing of forearms that would, according to the latest addition to my golf library, transform my natural fade-slice into a piercing right-to-left shape. It was sunny and the emerald-green fairway looked strangely wide and inviting.

Immaculately prepared and quietly confident, I relaxed, then swung well within myself, tracing a wide arc around my body. The clubhead rose and fell, accelerating smoothly. I anticipated the crisp impact of the ball firing off the face like a tracer bullet.

There was a dull, muffled thud, followed by an explosion of mud and grass. The ball struggled unwillingly into the air then, like a bird fatally winged by a volley of buckshot, banked sharply into the trees, the first crack echoed by a second and third as my Titleist pin-balled between the trunks.

'Sod it,' I said.

It would take a further three shots, one hacked, one sliced and one skulled, to reach the green, followed by a plethora of putts, the penultimate effort drifting apologetically off line from 2½ feet. Andrew, my thirteen-year-old chicken drumstick of a nephew, smirked undiplomatically through gleaming teeth braces.

'Triple bogey!' he broadcast, unnecessarily loudly, in his as yet unbroken falsetto.

As if I had somehow managed to lose count! For a moment, I considered supplementing his orthodontic metalwork with a well-placed three-iron, but I would probably have missed anyway. The overriding sense was of disgust and self-loathing.

Why that particular shot, or indeed that hole, hurt so much I do not know. I had hit worse. Once, on a course near Colchester, I smashed a drive flush into a rubbish bin 10 yards ahead of me. There was a huge, reverberating clang, the ball fizzed back past my shins and embedded itself into a large pile of rotting leaves.

In India, just north of New Delhi, I hooked three successive tee-shots into a field of out-of-bounds and increasingly concerned water buffalo.

This time, though, it was different. I had had enough.

I rehearsed my excuses as I retreated to the bar, accompanied by two of my three brothers and the willowy, victorious Andrew and his precocious sixteen-over-par scorecard. I had lurched militarily, left-right-left-right, from rough to bunker and back again, on the way to a bruising 26 over. But it was, after all, only my second game after a long break. And on a course I didn't know. And my arthritic left ankle had throbbed painfully. And . . .

But something had snapped. My golf had got beyond a joke. Supposedly, it was fun. It was meant to be beautiful. The occasion – an annual match in memory of Dad, who had died the year before – was meant to bring us all together, not reduce me to such depths of isolated resentment.

It was time for a rethink. It was time to give up. Or rather, golf had just given up on me.

TWO
ALL WASHED UP

'Golf is an ideal diversion, but a ruinous disease'
— *Bertie Forbes*

'Can I have a word?' he whispered from the corner of his mouth as, stern-faced and spectre-like, he glided past my desk.

I knew what was coming. I shadowed my boss into his goldfish-bowl of an office with the demeanour of a man mounting the scaffold. My colleagues pretended not to notice but I felt their eyes burning holes in my back.

There was no great preamble, not so much as a: 'So how are you? Family? Daughter? What are you doing for Christmas? Are you feeling any better?'

No, just: 'As you know, Tony, we've been asked to make a number of redundancies . . . '

I walked out five minutes later, in my late forties, jobless, all washed up. It was 18 December 2005.

Actually, it wasn't quite like that.

To be truthful, my boss was doing me a favour in ushering me towards the door, a generous pay-off in hand. I'd been unwell for months – my Post-Viral Fatigue had returned with a vengeance – my family life was a mess and, capping it all, Reuters's London sports desk was switching to evening work.

Clearly I wouldn't be able to cope with the new hours – it

was tough enough just staying awake during the day. And when would I see my daughter and my wife? Something had to give. I would probably have been laid off eventually due to ill health anyway. And, after twenty years, I was beginning to tire of sports writing. I'd studied French and German language, literature and linguistics at university only to choose – to my father's wry amusement – to spend my time scribbling down every mould-breaking insight offered up by Beckham and Co. ('It's a game of two halves, obviously I'm delighted, the lads showed real character . . .')

Perhaps Dad had been right. I felt deflated and burnt out by the banality of it all. The offer of voluntary redundancy seemed the best option, even if I returned home on the train that evening gnawing at any fingernail within reach.

My wife Jan, though, was upbeat. It made perfect sense. She'd return to full-time work and I'd become a house husband while recovering my health. I'd freelance, in between the ironing, shopping and darning. I'd grow green fingers, produce succulent organic vegetables and serve up dishes to die for (in that, she was almost right – I did, indeed, produce a number of dishes to die from). We'd see more of each other, our six-year-old daughter Emma would no longer be orphaned to our careers and life would become a soft-focus idyll.

There were a few formalities to complete first. I was wheeled before an ashen-faced redundancy consultant. He wore an undertaker's suit and spoke in sombre tones, as if intent on avoiding offence. The room seemed colder than usual. Was I really sure what I was doing? Did I fully understand the consequences? Redundancy pay-offs rarely last as long as one might imagine, he muttered dolefully. I had to write down my personal pros and cons on some sort of grid.

I began with the cons. 'Overweight. Ill. Arthritic.' I dithered, then left the pros section blank.

They threw me a going-away party. After a few drinks I cheered up. Perhaps it was the wine, but I began to feel more sorry for my colleagues than they for me. I received a giant farewell card, a couple of packages were thrust into my hands and I was gently pushed off in the direction of the Underground. On the way home I opened my gifts. Two books. The first was on cricket, the second on golf instruction.

'Typical,' I thought. 'I gave the game up a couple of years ago and nobody noticed.' Still. It would fetch the price of a pint on eBay. I got home late and merrily crumpled.

The following months were spent trudging in and out of doctors' surgeries and lying in hot baths, staring blankly at the cracked tiles above my toes. I trekked to and from school, reluctant daughter in tow. I shouted obscenities at Delia Smith recipes (particularly the broccoli soufflé). The doctors told me what I already knew. I was overweight, arthritic and ill. And, most pertinently, there was no proven cure for my fatigue. I should accept the condition, sleep, eat healthily, avoid stress and cut back on alcohol. I lay back in the bath, a beer and a packet of chocolate biscuits on the side, and thought that, all in all, three out of five wasn't bad.

I don't know exactly when I came across that golf book again. Our house, under my jurisdiction, is not the tidiest. Actually, it's a bombsite. But one day I tripped over it while fighting with the Dyson. I flopped on to the sofa, grateful for an alibi, and flicked open *The Swing Factory*.

Perhaps it was fate. It opened on page 94.

I'm sure books have changed lives before. In my case, one single sentence was enough. Well, perhaps it didn't quite change my life. But it promised to transform at least a year of it.

There it was, as clear as day. 'The wrists must not roll.'

What?!?

Rolling wrists had been a fundamental tenet of my less-than-glorious five-year golf career. They'd been a building block. I'm sure I'd learnt to do it from some out-of-print Nick Faldo book. Surely, surely he'd compared the roll of the left wrist through impact to a rasping backhand, topspin table tennis shot? Faldo had won six Majors, dammit! Of course wrists rolled! Yet here were Steve Gould and D.J. Wilkinson, the brains behind *The Swing Factory* and the owners of the Knightsbridge Golf School, preaching the very opposite.

Were they maintaining that I'd based my entire golfing philosophy on a misconception? Were they seriously suggesting that I'd never, ever, had the remotest of chances of hitting the ball straight?

I was not having this. Somebody was propagating malicious nonsense. This needed sorting out immediately. Ideally, I would have liked to get hold of Faldo. By the neck, preferably. But that seemed improbable. He's 6ft 3in tall, and spends much of his time making pertinent asides on American television. I'm 5ft 8¼in and shrinking, and spend most of mine staring inanely at UK daytime television. I would have to make do with Gould and Wilkinson. I would go and give them a piece of my mind.

THREE
I BLAME CHARLIE BROWN

'Playing the game, I have learned the meaning of humility. It has given me an understanding of the futility of human effort'

—*Abba Eban*

To be honest, I've never excelled at anything much. Golf's the rule rather than the exception.

My mum, with justification, blames Charlie Brown. While still in shorts, I remember her presenting me with a cartoon-strip depicting Schulz's character climbing a tree, flying a kite, drawing and playing baseball while his soul-mate Lucy commentates: 'The trouble with you, Charlie Brown . . . is that you never . . . concentrate on . . . one thing at a time.'

'That's you,' said Mum. She thought I was too much of an all-rounder for my own good. She overestimated me, of course, like all loving mothers should. I was an all-rounder only in my mediocrity. It has never bothered me unduly. We can't all be naturally talented. If I've ever got anywhere, it's been through dogged effort. I belong to the Fraternity of One-Paced Triers.

I learnt this young. My elder brother Martin understood everything, remembered everything and got 'A's for everything. I didn't, however much I sweated. And boy, did I perspire. Looking back, I sometimes wish I'd tried a little less hard and had a little bit more fun along the way. My bloody-mindedness – and fluent French, gifted me via a Belgium-based childhood – got me to Worcester College at Oxford University but that also remains a regret. Having over-reached myself to get there, I spent the next four years paddling furiously to keep my head above water. I would have been far happier floating quietly along some educational backwater. Perhaps, subconsciously, I'd been trying to emulate Martin, who breezed into Oxford with a scholarship and breezed out again on the way to a brilliant career.

Boarding school had been different. There, I'd been a large sprat in a small pond. They even made me head boy. I regarded myself as something of a sportsman. For a few matches I opened the batting for the cricket 1st XI with one Chris Broad, who went on to make a name for himself. I, though, had reached my zenith. I got Gloucestershire under-19 county trials and got found out.

University confirmed my limitations. I'm led to believe that I played a college rugby game against Stuart Barnes, although I never got close enough to confirm his identity. Barnes, like Broad, went on to play for England. I did not.

I was equally mundane educationally. I shared German tutorials with a delightful toff called Bill. When he read out his complex, multi-layered essays, resplendent with eclectic references to politics, history, art and philosophy, our professor, Frank Lamport, would screw up his face in concentration and delight. When it was my turn he just screwed up his face. Comically, Bill thought I was the genius. He'd never experienced an ordinary, A-to-B thought in his life. I'd say something mundane and he'd clap his hands in delight as if I'd just split the atom. Bill went on to get a brilliant first. I did not.

Thus when I took up golf I did so without expectation. By then I'd failed in my first job in marketing and in my second in sales. I'd done better as a journalist but felt I'd found my rightful station. I was a well-meaning low-flyer. In my favour, I possessed a capacity for hard work and half-decent presentational skills. I remember the men at Unilever, my first employers, fretting that I could sound so accomplished in interviews but perform so weakly in IQ tests. Basically, I could bluff.

Bluffing with golf clubs, though, gets you only so far.

As a boy, there'd been the odd visit to the pitch-and-putt with Dad, and, as a young man, a few wayward range sessions. In 1997 I bought a set of second-hand clubs, while working for Agence France Presse, an international news agency, in India. I was rapidly approaching forty – both in age and waist measurement. My left ankle, courtesy of a long series of rugby injuries (the consequence of running slower than open-side flankers), no longer functioned properly. Golf seemed a good way to mix socially while pretending to be active. It wasn't sport as such. It was a good drinking session spoiled.

Twice a month we'd thrash agriculturally around a weed-ridden course on the edge of New Delhi before retiring for cold beers. It was a rather exotic introduction to the game. Rose-ringed parakeets and bee-eaters flitted around the greens, wild dogs took sand baths in bunkers and ponderous buffalo invaded the water hazards. The local villagers, squatting in the shade, grinned as we dug mad-dog divots in the spiralling summer temperatures.

My favourite hole was the 14th. Superficially, it was a straight, featureless par four with an out-of-bounds fence defining the right edge of the fairway. It belied those first appearances, however. As well-grooved slicers, we habitually carved our drives into the adjoining field. Within seconds, the ball would be snapped up by the gnarled hands of the arid plot's octogenarian, turbaned owner. Once, our caddies informed us, he and his pair of oxen had eked out an arduous living tilling the land. Now the three companions chewed grass contentedly together in the quiet shadow of a tree, while awaiting a more lucrative harvest.

The old man had learnt his new trade quickly. 'Ten rupees?' he'd cackle derisorily in Hindi as the British High Commissioner's personal secretary opened negotiations for the return of his ball. 'You're joking! It's one of the new Titleists, giving you both extra feel and distance. At least five of the world's top twenty are using it. Let's say forty.'

Occasionally, I played at the Army Golf Club. It was a picturesque course, by the Delhi Cantt railway station, but it had far too many eucalyptus, banyan and laburnum trees for my taste. I spent a whole year lost among them, while being scrutinised by the mockery of vultures massed in their higher branches (on the presumption, presumably, that a creature burdened with such a sickly-looking golf swing must already be deep into its death throes).

My brother Matthew, a single-handicap golfer, came on holiday and we squeezed in a round. I played the game of my life for a personal-best 22 over. I awaited his approval.

'Your swing? Well, look Tony, to be honest, it's . . . it's . . . it's pretty crap really,' he informed me.

This would not be the last time I'd hear such a damning verdict.

My three brothers had all taken up golf earlier. Matthew, an artist, led the field. Martin, the multi-millionaire businessman, and Roger, the actor, were less textbook but cannily effective, each playing to around 15. I'm not sure I had any ambitions of playing regularly, much less of taking them on, until I returned to France in 1999.

My mid-life crisis, and my interest in the game – the two were closely linked – began soon after. My left ankle joint, full of bone fragments, had locked. I was wheeled into a Parisian operating theatre where the surgeons cut open my lower leg, drilled out some bone and transplanted it into the ankle. The surgery cured the locking but also restricted my ankle movement. I was middle-aged, depressed, arthritic and falling apart. Recuperating, I realised that my sporting days were over. It was golf or nothing.

Soon after, Jan and I returned to London to be closer to our families. We bought a ramshackle terraced house near Brixton and gave ourselves five years to make it habitable. Within two, and out of the blue, Emma May (or Mayhem, as she became known) was born. Within three more years, worried about the inclusion of glue-sniffing as a core subject in the local curriculum, we had fled the capital.

In between the DIY and the nappies, I had made my first concerted, unsuccessful effort to get the hang of golf. I took regular beatings from my siblings. I swung a club in the living room, hacking out chunks of mantelpiece. I went to the range and the local golf course. I would take to the 1st tee with hope, a dodgy grip and a flat swing and return hours later with only my misplaced enthusiasm intact. Despite the wide fairways I never beat 18 over par. Most of the time it was a lot less handsome than that.

A strange thing, however, transpired. The worse I performed, the more emotionally ensnared I became. I played angry, frustrated golf, but kept going back. It was love-hate. Mostly hate. Golf tortured and teased me like an old man's mistress. Like all hopelessly handicapped golfers, I somehow drew solace from the one passable shot per outing, convincing myself that it, and not the other ninety-nine, was the true reflection of my abilities.

It took Andrew, on that fateful day in 2004, to bring me to my senses — golf simply wasn't for me — just as it would take redundancy, ill health and page 94 to persuade me to offer the game one final chance of taking me seriously.

FOUR
ONE FINAL MULLIGAN

'One minute you're bleeding. The next minute you're haemorrhaging. The next minute you're painting the Mona Lisa'

— Mac O'Grady

30 September 2006, Day 1: On the face of it, just another day. To me though, it's much, much more. It's Year Zero. The Opening Scene. One of 365. It's the start of my golf year.

Not that anybody notices. Jan stumbles out into the 6 a.m. darkness to join the London-bound Trail of the Living Dead. Emma stares puffy-eyed at the television while I wrestle my way out of the duvet. She splashes through a bowl of sugar, criticises my ham-fisted efforts at pigtails, sucks her thumb defiantly and refuses to practise her three times table.

Back home after school drop-off — 'Free!' I exclaim, drawing stares of stony disapproval from the VSPMs (Very Serious Playground Mums) — I write out my daily 'Things To Do' on the back of an envelope.

1) Emma's school friend Holly for tea. Or is it Millie? Or Ellie or Jade? Anyway, remember to pick her up this time (underlined twice). If in doubt, pick them all up and blame their sleep-deprived mothers for forgetting.

2) Shop – mini pittas, broccoli (Emma), houmous (Jan), chocolate biscuits (me – find a better hiding place).
3) Mow lawn (at least the part nearest the house).
4) 40 quid from hole in wall.
5) Overdue gas bill (again).
6) Join golf club.

It's taken me ten months since losing my job to get to the starting line. I spent the first four in bed, my Post-Viral Fatigue knocking me senseless three times a day, for two hours at a stretch. I gradually improved to an hour's sleep, twice a day. That made space for a little freelance work. Then there's the housework, the cooking, the gardening, the you-name-it-why-haven't-you-done-it-honestly-Tony-you're-bloody-useless. Something always gets in the way. By now, however, I've run out of excuses. It's time to give myself one final mulligan. I sit down one evening, in the full-bodied company of a bottle of red, and set my goals.

'I pledge,' I write, 'to play decent golf within twelve months. And drive a ball 300 yards (downhill and downwind along Tarmac, if necessary). And get an eagle. And beat my brothers. Oh, and lose weight. Or else I'm giving up. For good.'

Hm . . . too vague.

'I pledge,' I re-write, 'that I will play off a single-figure handicap within twelve months. And drive a ball 300 yards. And . . . '

No . . . too ambitious.

'I pledge,' I re-re-write, 'to play one round – no, make that two, to prove the point – in single figures within twelve months. Off the yellow tees. And drive . . . '

That seems reasonable. Single figures is real golf; 24

over is hacking, 18 borderline incompetent, 14 over no man's land.

For a while, I admit, I'd dreamt of something altogether grander. What about getting down to scratch within twelve months? I'd attend golf schools in the United States, I'd meet golf obsessives in Japan, I'd phone up Leadbetter, we'd get together now and then, and I'd play St Andrews and Augusta. Surely Jan would agree? Just for one year? She'd just have to work a little more overtime, that's all.

But no. There's real life to consider. I'm The Man In The Street. Men In The Street don't get to meet Leadbetter or play Augusta. A couple of single-figure handicap rounds will have to suffice for someone without a clue, without direction, without a waist, who hasn't swung in anger for three years and who must remember to pick up Holly and/or Millie/Ellie/Jade, go shopping, sort out gas bills and mow the parts of the lawn that She-Who-Must-Be-Placated is most likely to inspect.

St Andrews? No, I'm not going anywhere. I'm not going to get any further than Lindfield Primary School. As for free time, I reckon I might manage an hour a day, five days a week. That will have to be enough. I'll represent washed-up, ageing hackers everywhere. If I can do it, what with my dodgy ankle and my daily doziness, anybody can. If I can't, they should throw their clubs into the nearest water hazard along with me and find something better to do. Sure, I'm slightly kitchen-bound, but I'll do my research on the Internet. If I need to get hold of Leadbetter, it'll have to be by email.

So what's the plan?

Ask anyone who knows me and I hope they'd say that, deep down, I'm an enthusiast (even if my fatigue, coupled with the

OAP ankle, have done their best to turn me prematurely embittered). They'd say I'm prone to speak and act without engaging my brain. The sort who assembles Ikea furniture inside out before resorting to the instructions.

This time, though, I take serious stock. This time I want a cause. And I want a method.

Why exactly am I doing this? And how to go about it?

Why? That's complicated. There's Jan's 'why'. She thinks I need a year to regain my health. Her family come from solid Somerset stock. They believe in the medicinal properties of poaching pheasants and ferreting rabbits while going for 10-mile hikes. What better way to get me back on my feet than to trudge around in the fresh air for twelve months? The only bit that doesn't make sense to her is what she refers to as 'the bat and the little white ball'.

Then there's my 'why'. Fundamentally, I'd like to cheer up. I've been pretty grumpy for, well, about ten years, give or take. I'd like to feel better, too. And, thirdly, I'd like to hit a few good golf shots.

Can the game cure Post-Viral Fatigue and the Male Mid-life Crisis in one swoop? Well, it can't do worse than the acupuncture and herbal remedies I've been prescribed over the years. And why shouldn't golf make me smile? OK, so most of my shots are a source of anguish, but surely I'll improve? This should be fun. Every golfer on earth would swap their spouse, children and even, perhaps, their favourite club for such an opportunity.

I mean, there's nothing better than a pure strike of a golf ball. Really. Nothing. Even I know that. I am not sure a golfer can ever convey to a non-believer the feeling of unadulterated joy stemming from one of those all-too-rare successes.

A good golf shot, they say, represents the most fun you can have with clothes on.

After an unending string of abominations, the planets and constellations suddenly click into alignment. You swing smoothly. You hit down into the back of the ball with the minimum of effort and launch it on a fizzing, piercing trajectory that slices the sky in two. Time freezes. Then the white dot stalls, falls, checks on the green and rolls inexorably towards the hole. No one breathes. Everything is perfect . . . until your playing partners puncture the stillness.

'You jammy bastard!' they scream.

And they're right, of course. The planets move on, you miss the 4-foot putt and chunk your next shot into the lake, just as you did last week and will no doubt do the next. But no one can take that one moment away. For weeks, it makes you smile in overcrowded trains and slow-moving supermarket queues.

Or, as Arnold Palmer once put it: 'What other people may find in poetry or art museums, I find in the flight of a good drive.'

Perhaps there's even more to my taking up the game again. Perhaps I have something to prove. Sure, I'd love to beat my three brothers, after all those abject humiliations. I may not be as fist-pumpingly competitive as I once was, but a little retribution never goes amiss. But I'd also like to prove that, after years of physical and mental slippage, there's still life in the old dog. Surely I can learn a few new tricks? Perhaps it will give me a little more confidence and energy to get off my expanding backside? When was the last time I gave anything a really decent go?

Jan shrugs her shoulders. 'You're over-complicating, as usual. It's a silly, pointless game,' she says. 'Just go and get some fresh air.'

But if a single, fundamental reason exists for trying to master golf, it probably stems from a sense of intrigue.

I've long been fascinated by the game's greatest conundrum. Statistics suggest the average golf handicap has failed to improve in thirty-odd years. An Internet trawl reveals that the average eighteen-hole score for men is 95 and 106 for women. And that despite the proliferation of NASA-technology clubs with heads as big as bungalows, revolutionary laser-guided training aids, sixty-frames-a-second video analysis and 'guaranteed' breakthroughs championed by high-profile coaches and players.

How can this be possible? And why do we put up with it?

I spent six thankless years as an integral part of those statistics. I'm typical of this sadly deluded race. I hack, you hack, he, she or it hacks, we hack, we have always hacked and we always will.

Surely it must be easier than this?

As for an answer to the game's central puzzle, well, there seem to be three possibilities. We are not improving because:

a) golf is infernally difficult or
b) it is badly taught or
c) it is badly learnt.

So that's the 'why'. What about the 'how'?

This, I believe, is where I've always gone astray. There's never been a method to my madness. It's time to don my Sherlock Holmes deerstalker.

I conclude that the secret to learning golf must lie in one of two places – it's either in Knightsbridge, with Gould and Wilkinson . . . or in my garage.

I begin with the garage. I rummage through a stack of

mildewed packing cases, untouched since our last house move. They contain forty-two golf magazines, twenty-three books and ten videos, each full of information on how to stand, grip, swing, putt, chip, pitch, and eat bananas and nuts and drink plenty of water. Do what you're told, they coo, and you'll play like Hogan, Nicklaus or Woods.

Buried somewhere in this cornucopia must surely lie The Golden Nugget, that tip, training aid or philosophy which will realise my potential. I must have overlooked it first time around, that's all. It's merely a matter of being meticulous.

Not that everything is as clear as I'd wish. Some books make as much sense as Chinese calligraphy. The more I read, the less I understand. I mean, what exactly is a 'reverse pivot', 'wrist pronation' and the 'moment of inertia'?

While searching for the secret, I decide I also need to make a practical start.

In London, years back, I'd visited the range regularly but played rarely. My practice had been characterised by boomerang drives and thunderous bouts of swearing. Increasingly exasperated, I'd batter my way through three buckets of balls, spraying wildly and at the speed of light, any swing thoughts long gone. All I wanted was to get rid of the evidence and escape incognito.

There'd been a few lessons — I even attended a three-day residential course — but nothing had transformed me into the player I dreamt of becoming. Like all hackers, I'd been seduced by new equipment. Until 2003 I played with a battered 'spoon' made out of bamboo twine and sheep horn which had once belonged to a Scottish crofter. Then I stumbled into a TaylorMade demonstration and persuaded myself to double our mortgage with a new set of woods.

The new clubs changed things markedly. Henceforth, I hit the ball even further out of bounds.

Consistency was my problem. My friends either sliced, hooked or missed the ball altogether, but at least they had a bread-and-butter shot. At least there was predictability to the proceedings. I'd hoik left with my first, carve right with the second, duff the third and gouge out a trench requiring planning permission with the fourth. I was capable of anything, and at any time. I got complimented on my swing on occasions. Nobody, however, complimented me on my scores.

I suppose I bear a golfing grudge. I always felt I should be a decent player. I tried. I really did. But it seemed as if there were some dark conspiracy afoot. I'd admit to one weakness only – I couldn't pitch, chip or putt. Or play out of bunkers. OK, four weaknesses. I know these are cardinal sins. But, to be frank, chipping's mere fiddling and putting's piffling. I draw joy from well-struck woods and irons. They speak to my soul. Putts don't say anything at all. They're mute.

So that's the plan. Study hard, work hard. Perhaps chip and putt a bit more. I've always talked a great game but never walked one but this time things will be different.

Find a club. Find a teacher. Find the secret.

I phone up the Knightsbridge Golf School, whose two senior coaches co-authored *The Swing Factory*. I book a lesson.

Golf, here I come. For one final swing.

FIVE
NOT EXACTLY ERNIE

'I suppose I have a highly developed capacity for self-delusion, so it's no problem for me to believe that I'm somebody else'

— *Daniel Day-Lewis*

Weight: 13st 10lb
Waist measurement: 38–39in
Diet: Bread. Chocolate biscuits. My daughter's left-over fish fingers/chicken nuggets/chips.
Weekly alcohol intake: 2¼ bottles of red wine and three gottles of geer.
Chronic fatigue: 2 hours sleep a day.
Handicap: To be determined.
Rounds played: 0
Range balls hit: 0
Self-belief: 10/10

1 October, Day 2: 363 days, 13 hours, 30 minutes to go.
My challenge proper begins at 10.30 on an overcast morning at Paxhill Park Golf Club.

I should have prepared better but I only remember to make Emma's school lunch at the last minute. At least I clean my clubs and succeed, after a protracted archaeological dig, in clearing my golf shoes of their 4-inch crust of antediluvian mud. I extricate a black, desiccated banana, a pair of mould-ravaged socks and something I cannot quite identify from my golf bag, as well as £4.36 in loose change. Once at the course, four minutes early, I throw myself into a brisk, optimistic warm-up, confident that a few stretches and a cracking of knuckles should suffice.

As the club's newest member, I must hand in three cards for an official handicap, something I have never previously possessed. Secretly, I'm confident. Paxhill is fairly short at around 6,000 yards, pretty straight and wide. It is what it is – basic and honest, with no hidden tricks. The greens are on the slow side of pedestrian. A round of 18 over doesn't seem out of the question.

And so I open my shoulders and my account. Memorably, as it turns out. In a commendable show of maturity, I opt for my three-wood rather than the driver, taking the longest of two fairway bunkers, at 220 yards, out of play. I needn't have worried. I miss the trap by 215 yards. The ball, topped into the turf, bounces off the front of the tee before dying of embarrassment in a thick collar of grass.

I am still short of the fairway after my second, an ugly, off-balanced hack, then I hook a five-iron into the rough. Two shots later and I'm on the green. Three putts later and I'm in the hole. Quadruple bogey.

James Crawshaw, a professional club-maker and my playing partner, keeps his counsel. I wish I hadn't shared my golfing ambitions with him. He has the decency not to laugh, but holds his hand to his mouth, so I can't be quite sure. James is tall and lean and knowing. He hits the ball in crisp straight lines. He plays off 12 but looks better than that to my untutored eye. I am short and bulging in all the wrong places and I hit round chicanes. Three hours later I reach the clubhouse with a score of 103 – 32 over par. I have hit a lot of fairways, most of them belonging to neighbouring holes and some to neighbouring courses. I hooked, sliced, lost four balls and three-putted four or five times. Or had I five-putted three or four times? A solitary par stood out amid the carnage.

I buy James a stiff drink. He clearly needs one.

'Obviously I'm a bit rusty . . .' I begin in mitigation.

He pretends to listen but suddenly remembers a prior engagement. Leaving, he suggests a round in single figures may be pushing it a bit but adds that he thinks I have something. He does not specify what. Polio, probably.

This is not going to be as easy as I'd imagined.

I retire to my laptop and discover that the statistics are not in my favour.

A golf ball, apparently, weighs 1.62oz and has a diameter of 1.68in. Its flight characteristics are affected by changes in wind direction, temperature or humidity. It must be hit with a club of between 3–4ft in length, with a head measuring approximately 1.8in high and 3in wide. That head moves at around 90mph at impact (unless you are Tiger Woods, in which case it tends to be 125, or unless you are me, in which case it tends to be nearer 12.5). The ball stays on the clubface for 0.00045 seconds. The golf swing, from takeaway to impact, lasts around one second.

Modern golf courses occupy about 150 acres. Somewhere in this undulating expanse are eighteen holes, measuring 4¼in across. Effectively, you're looking for eighteen jam jars within 726,000 square yards. To make things more interesting, there are bunkers, trees, long grass, water hazards and Paxhill Park Veterans in the way.

The biggest variable, though, is the human body. Robots

excel at golf because they are rigid and repeat identical actions. The human frame is less dependable. It has more than 230 joints, many of which can move in a variety of directions and most of which influence at least one part of the golf swing.

One last thought. Golf is counter-intuitive. It's a game of opposites. You hit down to hit the ball up, you swing left and the ball curves right and you swing easier to make the ball go further. The lowest score wins. The winner pays for the drinks.

Apart from that, it's pretty simple.

Within a fortnight, I'll have been awarded a handicap of 24. It could have been worse. I averaged 28 for those three outings. How does that make me a 24? I've never really understood the vagaries of handicapping. The important thing is that I'm under way.

Day 5: Emma is not happy with 'The Great House Husband Experiment'. I burnt her fish fingers again last night. The real crime, though, is that I'm not Jan. Emma weeps bitterly when Mum sets off for work and she leaps up and down with excitement on her return. Emma tells me I'm not as good at cuddling. She's right. I'm rubbish. At cuddling, at cooking, at being Mum. But there's no alternative. Tell that to an angry six-year-old. I try to bribe my way into her affections with chocolate and ice cream. She looks directly at me, knowing she has gained the upper hand, and asks for seconds without saying 'please'.

Day 6: I turn up for an appointment with an ME consultant. ME, as in Myalgic Encephalopathy. Or CFS (Chronic Fatigue Syndrome). Or PVFS (Post-Viral Fatigue Syndrome). Or

YLARTMYLGJPYTM, as in 'You Look All Right To Me, You Lazy Git, Just Pull Yourself Together Man' (my mother-in-law's sentiments).

I'm not too keen on these sort of chats. They invite self-pity. I'm good at self-pity, which is demoralising. And I know, and he knows, that there's no cure.

It crosses my mind that I suffer from a similar golfing affliction. No cure. The consultant must be a mind-reader because, within minutes, we're discussing golf rather than my sleeping habits. When I leave, I do so with *The Golf of Your Dreams*, by psychologist Bob Rotella, under my arm.

'Let me know how you go,' says the consultant.

Rotella argues that you should find a good teacher and stick with him. The man's clearly an idiot. I mean, surely you have to kiss a fair few frogs to find a prince? And how will I know which teacher to trust if they teach different things? It's a lottery.

Day 9: Emma's safely in school, studying volcanoes and the Siberian elk. Jan's safely in her office, editing dispatches from Mogadishu and Jerusalem. I'm carrying out job interviews.

Interview No. 1, 10 a.m. Burgess Hill golf range. The pro, Ben Lovell, is a nice guy. He's commentated for the BBC and Sky. He says my swing isn't bad, although the plane's a bit flat.

'You've got something to work with,' he says. He adjusts my grip and eases my right shoulder back to straighten my alignment. 'You could play off single figures with a bit of work,' he concludes.

Mysteriously, I hit the ball better with him there. There's no mention of a secret.

Interview No. 2, 11.30 a.m. Paxhill. Bernard Firkins is an

obvious choice, as the club pro. He overhauls my chipping. My wrists are not working right, he says, and I come over the top, either 'smothering' low and left or cutting right. Golf, he tells me, is a simple game. He's confident my challenge will succeed. I hit the ball better than I normally do. No secret.

Interview No. 3, 1 p.m. Haywards Heath Golf Club. Alastair Malins, one of the assistant pros, looks too young to be let out on his own after dark. He examines my swing on video and says my hands are too close to my body at address. A few rounds in single figures will be tough but it's possible. I hit the ball better. Again, no secret.

They clearly all know what they're talking about. They're all qualified teachers and scratch golfers and seem interested in what I'm trying to do. Of the three, Malins seems the most technical and Firkins the most intuitive. How to choose? I'd hoped that one of them would be incompetent, incontinent, forget my name or have unbearably large facial warts, anything really, to give me a reason for declining his services.

More worrying is that I'm clearly doing lots of things wrong. I'd dreamt of having to iron out the one, single, solitary, minor suggestion of an idiosyncrasy in my swing – rather than the 1,862 fundamental flaws that actually exist – on the way to becoming instantaneously marvellous. This may require reconsideration. For starters, I have a suspect grip and deplorable wrists. Then there's how far away I stand from the ball and my pancake plane. And that's before I get anywhere near hitting the ball.

Day 11: I arrive at Knightsbridge Golf School for my first lesson. I ask for a formal interview with Messrs Gould and Wilkinson, to discuss their golfing philosophies. They're tied up with more important clients – actors, footballers, oil magnates, princes and potentates – so I begin with one of their assistant teachers, Andy Pharro.

First impressions? I don't like him very much. My daughter, who I have irresponsibly dragged along with me, having failed to find suitable childcare, likes Pharro a lot. She stares dreamily at him like a smitten teenager. Pharro is young, tanned, matinee-idol lithe and a fine golfer. He dresses all in black and has a luxuriant head of hair. I don't think I like him at all.

He's also a little forthright for my liking. I've met – and been mauled by – friendlier Rottweilers. Our relationship deteriorates rapidly. He watches a few swings, then shows me the video. To say that I'm shocked is an understatement. I'd expected Pharro to be agreeably surprised. Instead he looks glum. I see why.

The good news is that I'm holding the right end of the club. The bad? Well, I'm aiming a tad left – well, all right, a lot left – as if intent on slogging a mid-wicket six. My backswing's horribly flat, with my hands wrapping around my neck. In the downswing, my arms get stuck behind me and I sway violently towards the target in a last desperate attempt to connect clubhead to ball.

'Not exactly Ernie Els,' says Pharro.

I presume this is his idea of a joke. Considering how much I'm paying, I expected a little more sympathy. Fatally, however, I've asked him to be brutally straight with me. He is.

'Not great,' he adds. A pause. 'Actually, let's be honest, it's crap.'

Put another way, I'm too close to the ball at address, forcing my hands away from my thighs in the takeaway. At some point they have to renew their acquaintance with the rest of my body, so my left wrist rolls over 90 degrees and swivels the club back low behind my shoulders.

Then comes the moment of truth – impact. Pharro suggests three possible outcomes. A block right as I swing from in to out. Or, if I get wristy, a low hook. Or, if I launch myself at the ball, an over-the-top slice.

He's just described my three bread-and-butter shots. The evidence is there, on the video. I think of contesting the facts but opt sulkily instead for the Fifth Amendment.

'The fundamental problem is those rolling wrists,' adds Pharro. 'It's a common error. Nearly all bad players do it.'

Even I can see that my takeaway is setting off a fatal chain-reaction of errors and compensations. My swing begins badly, then gets worse. Pharro spends the lesson trying thanklessly to get me to re-adjust my wrists while bullying my body into previously uncharted territory. I'm not sure I learn much but I do succeed in straining a back muscle, which suggests a certain commitment.

I ask Pharro why, if my swing is so detestable, have my friends occasionally complimented me on it in the distant past.

'You've got one thing going for you,' he replies. 'Your rhythm is quite nice and you're not bad through impact. But I bet you don't have many single-figure handicap friends.'

'What does crap mean, Daddy?' Emma pipes up on the train home.

So it's decision time. I've consulted four teachers. Three are polite and local. The other is rude and a tedious train ride away. Emma has started doing drawings of him and his magnificent hair, and writing 'Andeee' in rather wobbly script during school spelling tests. So that cuts the choice down to three.

Except that it doesn't.

I mean, *The Swing Factory* is the sole reason for me taking up golf again. It's because of Gould and Wilkinson, and page 94. It's their philosophy or bust. And, on reflection, I decide that I rather enjoyed my first lesson with Pharro, perverse though that may sound. Look, let's face it – if you're playing off 24 then you're crap. Let's not get too precious.

Above all, it proved that there's enormous room for improvement. The video, however painful, may provide the necessary wake-up call. No wonder I've always struggled. My swing has been designed by committee and constructed from unwanted prosthetic left-overs. There's something South African about my swing after all, but it isn't Ernie Els. It's the golfing equivalent of a wildebeest.

The Knightsbridge School, based in a grand Georgian terrace, also appeals to me, despite my initial misgivings. I'd examined their website with trepidation. The school was right next to Harrods – not exactly my kind of corner shop. It catered for the rich and famous. So was it just an overpriced gimmick? And, if so, what the hell was I doing, entering the inner sanctum in Tesco jeans and a broccoli-and-carrot-stained Matalan top?

In reality, however, 47, Lowndes Road is far less intimidating.

The school was set up by Leslie King, a celebrated teacher who plied his trade from the late 1920s. I'd never heard of him but, in his favour, he'd taught the great British amateur Michael Bonallack and the evergreen American professional Juli Inkster.

It may seem bizarre that King chose to establish himself in a basement squash court in the heart of Knightsbridge. He reasoned, however, that, as an experienced golf teacher, he already knew all about ball flight. He wanted to concentrate on dissecting people's swings.

That made sense to me. Most of my golf had been played in living rooms and hallways. So I wasn't downcast when Pharro banned me from the range and told me to focus instead on the moves he was trying to introduce. Beginners and golf balls, he said, don't mix. I stuck religiously to this rule. For forty-eight hours at least.

Knightsbridge's other major attraction came in the contrasting shapes of Steve Gould and Dave Wilkinson. Both had worked with King and continue to believe passionately that his methods, devised almost a century before, are as relevant as ever.

They make an odd couple. Gould, hair unkempt and unruly, waves his hands about almost as fast and furiously as he talks. There must be Italian blood, although his vocabulary is decidedly Anglo-Saxon. Wilkinson, Trappist by nature, measures each word carefully before opening his mouth, shutting it again and opting to stay silent. At times he seems to merge into the walls.

Gould is the 'people's' man, while Wilkinson, I assume, is more of a theorist and the behind-the-scenes brains.

I ask for an audience. 'Anytime, anytime,' says Gould. 'Now? Now!' And as he begins talking in Gatling-gun bursts, Wilkinson slips noiselessly away.

'Magazine tips? Rubbish! Unless you already have a structured swing, there's no point,' Gould rat-tat-tats before I squeeze out a question.

'All they do is give you one fault to cure another! Gizmos? Bollocks. Half of them don't do what they say. It's just to sell stuff. Gurus? Look, anyone can teach a tour player. The tour player wins a tournament and everybody asks: "Who's he seeing?" Mr Whoever gets a reputation, brings out the DVD and video, etc, but he's never really taught players as bad as you. He's a good player who turned to teaching to make a living out of it, that's his sum knowledge. We've been here for fifty years, we see golfers of all standards. That's what gives you teaching ability. But it's not rocket science. Nine out of ten players make the same mistakes.'

There's a nano-second of a pause, or perhaps just a suggestion of a nano-second of a pause. Gould has gone blue, presumably due to lack of oxygen. I take my chance.

'Butwhydoyouthinkaveragehandicapshaven'tcomedownin thirtyyearsSteve?' I blurt out.

'The wrists, the wrists, they're all rolling their wrists!' comes the answer. 'If you want a secret, there it is!

'You've only got to learn two or three things, Lord Antony (I never get to the bottom of my nickname – do I sound posh? I certainly don't look it). You're carrying a lot of baggage. Look at this picture of Hugh Grant. Look at that great backswing position. But no, first let me tell you about Zola. Emile? Who's Emile? No, you idiot, Gianfranco. Now there was a football player! Chelsea? The only club there is! Now, when Gianfranco first came here . . . '

So I have my secret. Rolling wrists.

Knightsbridge Golf School, I knew, would be my sort of place. Over the next twelve months it was to become my favourite place of worship.

SIX

THREE GOLFING HEROES

'If they can make penicillin out of mouldy bread, they
can sure make something out of you'

— *Muhammad Ali*

Weight: 13st 11lb
Waist measurement: 39in
Diet: Marmite toast; black chocolate (full of antioxidants —
  Woman's Weekly); 24 ice lollies left over from summer and
  which Jan threatens to bin.
Alcohol: Much the same. Nothing to be ashamed of.
Chronic Fatigue: No change.
Official handicap: 24
Rounds: 3
Average score: 28 over
Longest drive: 220 yards (7 October, second handicap round,
  Paxhill, 3rd hole)
Number of eagles: 0
Range balls: 200
Self-belief: 1/10
And the secret of golf is . . . don't roll your wrists.

15 October, Day 16: 349 to go.

I'm not argumentative by nature. Or rather, I'm not rebellious
(I am, Jan informs me, wilfully argumentative). I'm small-c
conservative. But there's only so much practising without a
ball that a man can do. Pharro won't relent. He wants me to

repeat my takeaway continuously in a dark room while feeding on bread and water.

'Your wrists are your Achilles' heel,' he explains.

I overlook the anatomical confusion. I bow to his greater knowledge. I keep it up for a few more days. I move to the 8 o'clock position, come back, move to 8 o'clock, come back. But after spending most of your time at 8 o'clock it's surely natural to pine for 8.30? As for 9 o'clock, that would be just wild . . .

What Pharro doesn't know cannot hurt him. I'll sneak down to the club in the next few days. After all, I've an important match coming up.

Day 17: 7.23 a.m. I lose the first psychological battle of the day and eat four chocolate biscuits while preparing Emma's school lunch. I am caught in the act.

'Can I have a biscuit too, Daddy?'

'No, you can't. And I want you to eat up all your carrots and cucumber today.'

'But you . . .'

'Come on, come on! We'll be late and we haven't looked at your spellings yet,' I spray through crumbs as I frog-march her back to the table.

'You don't cuddle as well as Mummy . . .'

8.30 a.m. I find myself discussing the advantages of elasticated waistbands with one of the VSPMs. She's five months pregnant but noticeably slimmer than I (it's closer if I don't breathe).

8.55 a.m. Sainsbury's, for tonight's spag bol. Think about Dyson-ing front room but decide it'll pass muster. If it doesn't, I'll blame a blown fuse. Jan doesn't understand fuses.

Nor do I. Wash up. Cup of tea while watching Golf Channel. Some chap says there are eight causes of a slice. He should visit Burgess Hill range.

9.15 a.m. Paxhill. Thursday. Vets' Day. The course is packed with grunting, grey-haired dervishes. They flail wildly. I'm tempted to ask whether I, considering my enfeebled state of health, might join in. But it looks dangerous. I head for the range.

I joined Paxhill for several reasons. Crucially, there's no joining fee, no waiting list, you can take out a weekday membership and it's ten minutes from home. I've never been a member of a golf club before. My brother Roger warned that I might find it elitist, sexist and claustrophobic. I'd cross swords with people who insist on the right-coloured socks and turn apoplectic if someone parks in the wrong space, or fails to tug their forelock while addressing The Highly Venerable and Most Magnanimously Majestic Competitions Secretary.

Perhaps these places still exist, but Paxhill's not like that. It's immediately friendly, and appealingly shabby. A bit like me, I like to think. The bar is fuller than the course, the barman heralds from Turkey and can't pronounce 'etiquette', the clubhouse roof leaks and the greens look like a herd of wild horses have been galloping over them (actually, a horse from a neighbouring farm does regularly gallop over them, chased by a herd of indignant, wheezing Veterans. We cheer on the horse). The place has character, and characters – like the two gruff, inseparable brothers with strange haircuts – Tweedle Dum and Tweedle Dee, I christen them – who randomly play a few holes every day, never bothering to announce their arrival or departure.

My incompetence should blend in nicely.

The range, though, is the selling point. You bring your own balls and hit them to your heart's content. Best of all, there's nobody there. Ever. It's the same story in the clubhouse nets. When it rains, I retire there and whirl away undisturbed. Paxhill golfers scoff in the face of practice.

After forty-five minutes of uninspired perspiration, I return to the pro shop and run into James Crawshaw. The dervishes have dispersed, though lingering echoes of 'Fore!' and 'Ouch!' suggest they're still active in the vicinity. I pluck up courage and ask for a game.

'Fine,' he says, failing to conceal his reluctance.

After nine holes, I am 14 over and have lost the three shiny new balls purchased for the occasion. All of them begin right and keep going. I also mislay my new takeaway early in the round. Firkins intercepts me by the 10th tee and suggests I jettison all clubs above the six-iron.

'They're not doing you any good,' he says, confiscating half my set.

I get his gist immediately. The 10th is a short par four, with out-of-bounds right. In two of my three handicap rounds I sliced my drives deep into East Sussex. This time I hit a respectable six-iron, followed by another that dribbles up to the front of the green. I chip to 5 feet and hole the putt. Par. Bleeding heck. With no clubs.

It's not rocket science, of course. I cannot hit straight, so why am I even attempting to use 'The Big Dog' and its younger cousin 'Fairly Big Dog'? 'The woods are full of long drivers,' they say. A 24-handicapper with a driver is to golf what an L-plated novice in a Ferrari would be to Formula One. Over-ambitious and decidedly dangerous.

I end on 22 over. At times, standing on the tee of the par fives with my pop-gun six-iron, there's a feeling of emasculation. But I've learnt something. Course management is worth four shots a round. I'm probably a 20-handicapper already! James, meanwhile, has played to 9 over and is happy. I make him look rather good, I reason. I'll ask him for another game soon.

My first round bodes well for the upcoming GG (Graham Griffiths) Trophy. It's an event close to my heart because Graham, apart from having been a friend, remains one of my golfing heroes. I use the word 'hero' – and, indeed, the word 'golfing' – loosely. It probably reflects my idiosyncratic personality that, if asked to choose my perfect foursome, I'd make Graham an automatic first pick, followed by a gentleman called Neil McLellan and my dad. Hogan, Snead, Woods, Sorenstam? I'm sure they're all very pleasant. But you can keep them.

Admittedly, none of my choices had the game to grace an instruction manual – indeed, Dad didn't play at all, beyond occasional forays to the pitch-and-putt with his short-trousered sons. As for McLellan, I never met the man. But all three, when they were alive, embodied inspirational personal qualities. And boy, they'd have made a hilarious combination.

Graham, bluntly, was the worst golfer I have ever set eyes on.

Words fail to do justice to the singular method he devised to hang, draw and quarter the game. As fellow cricket writers at Reuters, Graham and I endeavoured to capture sporting situations as graphically and vividly as possible. So how to describe Graham the golfer? Well, he resembled an over-zealous axeman who, having cleaved off the toes of his right foot, now appeared hell-bent on inflicting similar self-mutilation to his left. During his swing Graham defied gravity in lifting his arms up past his right ear. From this improbable position he would lunge murderously before burying the clubhead deep into the ground. If the ball happened to get in the way, it might – on a fortuitous day – progress a few yards. Normally, it stayed exactly where it was. Driver, five-iron, sand-wedge, it did not matter much. The technique – and the result – remained the same.

Graham's post-shot routine – he chose not to entertain a pre-shot one – was equally memorable. Graham was the perfect gentleman when calm. Pencil thin, he combed his hair neat and flat and wore bow-ties and Conservative-blue sports jackets. For the most part, he was as pleasantly inoffensive as camomile tea. Allow him to discuss the merits of Bradman, Bedser or Sobers and you'd never meet a more genial fellow.

But below the surface bubbled a Vesuvian side. When playing golf, Graham kept his temper in check for about three shots – his first two air shots and the opening shank off the 1st tee. Thereafter the offending ball – and Graham never hit it far enough to lose it – became the target for an uninterrupted torrent of abuse and invective.

'Oh for goodness sake! Stupid effing ball, what's bloody wrong with it, it's going all over the place! I thought it looked out of shape when I bought it! Bloody American rubbish! You can't trust them to do anything right!' he'd explode while stomping down the fairway in wild, angry zigzags.

'Stupid, stupid, stupid game!' Graham would conclude on the 18th green, before storm-troopering into the bar. 'I don't know why I bother.'

And why did he? The whole process seemed so tortured. I

never understood his motivation. A beer or two later, however, and Graham's equilibrium had invariably been restored.

'What do you actually get out of golf, Graham?' I once had
the temerity to ask. 'Why don't you stick to cribbage or
croquet? Or, at least, get some lessons?'

Graham smiled back graciously and adjusted his spectacles
before replying: 'Goodness no, Tony. I just play for fun.'

If the Universe were just, Graham would still be hacking
divots out of the Croydon skyline. But, after taking early
retirement and buying himself a crimson-red sports car (he
was the sort of man you pictured in a Morris Minor), he fell ill.
He told us he had jaundice but within a few weeks he was dead.
Cancer of something or other. It still seems absurd.

I miss Graham. But I still chuckle at the memories. For me,
Graham represents golf's greatest, most enduring enigma –
the triumph of dogged, misplaced optimism over the most
damning of evidence.

There are echoes of Graham in McLellan's story, although I
re-tell it without authority and at third hand. McLellan came
to life for me in the national newspapers, shortly after his
death in 2005. I would have liked to meet him. I may consider
myself golf's Man In The Street but McLellan was arguably the
Everyman of all Everymen in terms of his unrequited passion.
A bachelor and merchant banker, he spent many hours of his
retirement trying to decode golf's mysteries. He failed. When
he passed away, he did so as a 19-handicapper.

McLellan was, by all accounts, a private man. If he had any
secrets, I'm sure they went to the grave with him. What he
could not take, however, was the extraordinary collection of
golfing paraphernalia unearthed at his home in Dunblane
in Scotland.

The cache, including more than 3,000 near-pristine clubs, was valued at around £50,000. Many of those sets had been used just once before being discarded for the next. None transformed his game.

McLellan may have been as wryly amused as anyone by his love of technological innovation. I entertained the idea of paying homage by playing his local course – in an even more mediocre a score than he would have managed. I was also keen to fit a personality to the story. But my interest was not encouraged by the admirably protective members at Dunblane Golf Club. They felt McLellan had been mocked by his press obituaries and closed ranks as tightly around him in death as they would have done in life.

So be it. Let sleeping golfers lie. He remains for me, however, a figure to revere. He wanted desperately to play good golf. He may have been misguided in placing such faith in technology, but he was not the first and will not be the last. The man remained true to his dream. 'Courage is going from failure to failure without losing enthusiasm,' Winston Churchill said. In which case McLellan was very courageous indeed. I like to think of him sitting alongside St Peter, discussing the pros and cons of square-headed drivers.

In contrast, my dad, John Patterson Lawrence, was no dreamer. He was far too sensible and temperate to have his story published in the papers. 'Moderation in all things,' was his mild-mannered mantra. He was quiet, wise and cultured, and he knew where his happiness lay. In retirement, he made a tactical retreat from what he perceived as an ever more dangerous and threatening world. He stopped watching the news. I think it frightened him.

He was happiest pottering about at home in rural Suffolk, in the safety of Mum's company. In his final years, he began going deaf but refused to consider a hearing aid. I think he was content in his isolation. When I was younger, and full of puppy-bounding enthusiasm, he used to laugh and say to me: 'You talk an awful lot, Tony, for someone with so little to say.' Perhaps he just felt he had done enough listening for one lifetime.

God knows why Dad never discovered golf. They'd have dovetailed perfectly. The game would never have frustrated him. He understood that life was not designed to be fair. He never lost his temper. The only time I heard him swear was when flattening his thumb with a hammer. As a young man, he had been an excellent sportsman – that would have helped his golf. He was good at mapping his way through crosswords – that would have helped too. And he was blessed with patience and perseverance. God knows what he'd have made of Graham, though.

I can still see Dad today, in the family kitchen, a chilled Dutch gin in hand, telling Mum: 'Mrs L, have I told you recently that I love you?'

He died unjustifiably young, seven years into retirement.

I wish we could have played golf together. I'd have enjoyed that. It's not that I had anything special to say to him. It's not that I have regrets. I know my dad loved me, even if he didn't choose to say it. I'd have liked to hang around with him, that's all – just him and me, for a whole eighteen holes. I'd have liked to watch. Perhaps, deep down, I feel I didn't get enough time with my father.

I imagine him in the middle of a fairway, sucking a Fisherman's Friend and eyeing up a seven-iron to a green bathed in evening sun, at peace with himself and his semi-reclusive world.

Dad would never have won the GG Trophy, though. It's a real challenge, especially if you have a modicum of talent. It's a wonderful event, devised by Graham's former colleagues and with a most satisfying set of rules;

1) 18 holes of strokeplay
2) try your very best
3) may the worst man/woman win.

Graham would have been tickled by the notion of the worst player lifting a trophy named after him. As for me, I have never won but I have contended. There's always been some spectacularly inept player, however, to trump me.

This year, though, I have a different agenda. I hope to play well. I hope to mark my year of golf by 'losing', and losing badly. I want to come last. I'm sure Graham would have approved.

Day 23: I don't play weekend golf. Jan often works on Saturday or Sunday, so my weekends are entirely Emma. Quality time. Bonding time. That's the theory. But there's only so much bonding you can do with a pink, pony-tailed Mayhem who watches *High School Musical* on a loop while combing Barbie and Ken's hair and who howls with injustice should you dare to check the cricket scores.

I've kept to the rules for six months. I've taxied her to horse riding and swimming, ballet rehearsals and drama. We've gone on picnics and adventures and had her friends round. Hundreds of them, every one pink and pony-tailed. But cracks are beginning to show. I feel I deserve a short break. I'd like to bond with myself.

So I ask a favour of Frank and Clare next door and Clare smiles and Frank tries to, through gritted teeth. They say yes, how lovely, of course they'll have her for a couple of hours. She can play with their tom-boy daughter Freyja while I escape to the golf range. Everything is arranged. But at the last minute Emma refuses to let go of my sleeve. I bluff.

'You'll have to come to the range with me then.'

Emma hates the range. Even more than vegetables. It's a master stroke.

'OK,' she says.

I know it's a bad idea but I go through with it. I sit her down in a chair, along with Sleeping Bag (a frayed bit of material she slept in as a toddler and to which she is now surgically attached) and Baby (a bald, misshapen, discoloured, unhygienic doll dating back even further) and a book about a lamb called Larry. I address my first ball.

'Is it time to go yet?' Emma squeaks.

I rush through my repertoire of tops, slices and duck hooks. Now Emma wants a try. Holding my nine-iron halfway down the shaft, she hits her first three shots 20 yards straight down the range. The professional smiles. It's clear who he feels is the brighter prospect.

Day 24: Step One accomplished! Eureka! I've mastered the takeaway! After some midnight practice sessions in front of the French windows, I no longer roll my wrists. I head back to Knightsbridge in search of Step Two.

'No, you're still doing it,' says Pharro, and we run through the same lesson again. Waste of money. The man's clearly an idiot.

Day 25: Lesson with Firkins. 'I've been watching you,' he begins. 'I don't think you should play full rounds at the moment.'

He gets me to chip again and says we'll build from there.

'You're rolling away from the ball. You're too handsy, too floppy. The swing's not tight enough.'

Handsy players, he explains, can get away with it by keeping their bodies still, while players who sway or slide can salvage shots by playing with neutral hands. I'm handsy, I sway and there's no salvaging.

Day 26: Lesson at Burgess Hill range. Lovell wants the club to come more from the inside into impact. 'Imagine a topspin forehand at tennis,' he says. I'm rubbish at tennis and I loathe Wimbledon.

Day 27: My first day of reckoning. I drive to Poult Wood, near Tonbridge, for the GG Trophy.

Dave arrives, then Mitch, who shouts 'Bloody cheat!' after spotting me on the putting green. 'Bacon sarnie and a cup of cha?' I decide not to mention my golf project. If warming up is cheating, what will Mitch make of lessons? Mitch, incidentally, is dressed more like a basketball player than a golfer but I don't mention it.

Dave, our host and a Reuters veteran, holds the trophy. I wouldn't say he modelled himself on Graham, but their swings have similarities. Dave, tall, greying and Roman-nosed, also carries about as much muscle bulk as a greenfly and he, too, starts with his weight firmly planted on his front foot. Somewhere during the downswing, though, he steps backwards, enabling him – on a good day – to catch ball rather than turf. There's another difference. Dave has no temper. He's studiously calm, like all good sub-editors should be. There are just the occasional, soft laments of 'Oh Dave!' I suppose he enjoys himself, after a fashion, although there are no obvious signs. Dave says he'll take lessons when he retires but I doubt it. I suspect he just likes walking among friends.

Mitch is less of a puzzle. I know lots of Mitches – good sportsmen, just beginning to fray at the edges ('Me? Fraying? Bollocks!') but still pretty fit. While I've all but given in to the ageing process, Mitch rages at his receding hairline. As in-your-face as Dave is out of it, he's taken up triathlons. He cycles to work, sitting at his desk enveloped in Lycra and with a helmet perched ridiculously on his head. The stats, though, put Mitch in my bracket – the confirmed 18- to 24-handicappers. He boosts that to 26 whenever money's involved.

His golfing flaw is simply diagnosed. Mitch is as tall as the Post Office Tower and likes to belt the ball. He doesn't so much play golf as attack it. And, with arms extending beyond his knees, it's full-on GBH. Sadly, direction can be an issue. I say 'sadly' but Mitch would not.

'Who wants to play patty-cake golf? Much better to unload your Big Bertha,' he argues. 'OK, the Devil's Deal is that a few balls will end up in the woods but that's a price worth paying for a 300-yarder.'

A lot of Mitch's balls end up in the woods, and I've yet to see a 300-yarder from him, but I'm not about to disabuse the great man. In some way, we're alike. We both love the long game and think putting's for wimps. But his best round of 10 over leaves me in the shade. He certainly has the unflappable temperament required. Mitch wears a permanent, unslippable smile.

The only time I remember him mildly irritated was when his wife, pregnant with their first child, phoned him during his lunch hour at the office to say her waters had broken.

'Bleedin' typical!' said Mitch. 'Can you believe it! I've only just started my lasagne!'

In one key area, however, we're polar opposites. I believe fundamentally that good golf must be more fun than bad golf. Much more fun. Inversely proportionally more fun. If one good shot per round is enjoyable, then ten a round must be twenty times better. So, if you're going to play, you simply must try to improve.

Mitch begs to differ.

'Practice?' he scoffs. 'Bleedin' boring! Tiger Woods says he'd still head to the range with 400 balls if you gave him the day off. What a bundle of fun he must be.'

Mitch believes belting's best, irrespective of circumstance. His game relies heavily on selective memory – the worse he plays, the more his occasional good shots stand out.

I'm paired with Mitch and Martyn, another of my former Reuters colleagues. Martyn combines Latin good looks, a quietly generous spirit and a complicated personal life – he's tried to explain it to me on a number of occasions but I always get lost in the twists and turns – with a neat-looking swing and a bad back. I remove the woods from my bag but decide, against Firkins' advice, to retain all the irons.

Mostly, we play to a similar standard but I ease away on the closing holes, mainly because of Martyn's misaligned lumbar region and Mitch's misplaced ambition.

Mitch, though, gets the last laugh. The 16th is a 291-yard par four, doglegging right. A solitary fairway bunker lies within 200 yards of the tee. Mitch unholsters his driver.

'Watch this – I'll cut it over the trap, around the corner, on to the green,' he declares.

I sigh theatrically.

Mitch snorts in defiance and, like a bull impatient for Pamplona, hurls himself forward in a flurry of arms and elbows. His ball fizzes 40 yards along the floor and into a thick bush.

Egged on and in direct contravention of his dapper appearance, Martyn opts for the same approach and shanks 25 yards forwards and 30 yards right. I take out my five-iron – 'Yer big girl's blouse, Lawrence!' – and hit 170 yards straight down the pipe.

There's no justice, though. I smooth a nine-iron to 10 feet and miss the birdie putt. Martyn and his perfectly ironed slacks are never seen again but Mitch hacks out of his rhododendron, tops a five-iron on to the green and holes a squirmy 35-footer for par. For a nano-second, he remains quietly dignified.

Then 'told you, you tart!' he guffaws. 'You just HAVE to use a driver here!'

The day ends in an upset. Dave is somehow beaten and hands over the trophy, for a year at least. We retire to the bar to discuss our glorious successes – 'Well, Tony goes with this pathetic five-iron but I decide to really hammer a . . . ' – and to raise our glasses to Graham.

I am delighted to be near the back of the field, with 19 over. I even get close to Laurie Morrison, a handy 18-handicapper. For half the drive home, it feels like a triumph. I've lost five shots in a month!

But it dawns on me that my progress has been based on an illusion. I'm still erratic. I still roll my wrists. I still crash. In removing my woods, all I've done is to put on a seatbelt and reduce the scale of the damage. Today I hit one ball out of bounds where normally I'd hit three. And there's been a high price to pay — an entire afternoon of baiting from Mitch The Marauder.

The bottom line? I still can't play.

SEVEN
ME AND MY MATE HUGH GRANT

'It isn't tying himself to one woman that a man dreads when he thinks of marrying. It's separating himself from all the others'

— *Helen Rowland*

Weight: 14st (Gawd. Unprecedented. But with shoes on, wallet and keys in my pocket).

Waist measurement: 39½in

Diet: Reduced carbohydrate intake (Atkins). More protein (Jan). A family-sized jumbo pack of crisps (six salt and vinegar, six cheese and onion, six BBQ) within forty-eight hours (Tony).

Alcohol: Less than John Daly.

Chronic Fatigue: 2 hours a day.

Rounds: 5

Official handicap: 24

Average score per round: 25 over

Eagles: 0

Longest drive: 230 yards (26 October, Poult Wood, 4th)

Range balls: 650

Self-belief: 2/10

And the secret of golf is . . . course management (if in doubt, watch Mitch, do opposite).

2 November, Day 33, 332 to go.

10 a.m. Train to London. I'm meeting Hugh Grant today. I've got it all worked out. We'll become the best of buddies. Blood

brothers. Mates. Sure, I know, it sounds implausible – Hollywood male lead bonds with overweight, sleepy house husband. But we share a common language.

We'll meet and I'll tell him my story and, despite himself, he'll be intrigued. There'll be an immediate connection. One of us will suggest playing a round or two, between film shoots, Oscars, Baftas and Emma's swimming and ballet. We'll exchange emails. After that, who knows? He's probably got holiday homes dotted around, so some sort of invitation isn't out of the question. He'll have other golfing partners, naturally, like Michael Douglas, Alice Cooper, Prince Andrew and Bill Clinton. Notwithstanding, I'll tell Jan to keep our holiday plans flexible for the next twelve months.

Hugh, you see, also takes lessons at Knightsbridge. Wilkinson says there's a lot of early Hugh in my swing. He wasn't much better than I am now – 'he had shockingly bad wrist roll and got his hands so far behind him that he had to loop them over his head to get back to impact' – but they sorted him out over a couple of years and reduced his handicap to 7. After a long break, he's back, playing off 5 and with more to come, according to Wilkinson.

It seems that Hugh and I are on the same golfing journey, even if he's quaffing champagne in first class next to Miss Universe while I'm swilling cheap lager next to the malfunctioning toilet at the back. If I watch Hugh's remodelled swing carefully, perhaps I'll pick up his secret. Five handicap – and a cameo in Hugh's next blockbuster – here I come . . .

12.15 p.m. On the train home. Didn't meet Hugh Grant. Wilkinson said he'd been held up. Something to do with the paparazzi and a baked beans tin, I think. Anyway, I had Emma to pick up from school and couldn't hang around. Perhaps we could try another day? Wilkinson said he'd pass on the message. I thought of interviewing Wilkinson instead but he'd slunk off.

As for my lesson, well . . .

'You're still rolling,' says The Rottweiler. I'm trapped in a golfing 'Groundhog Day'. I examine the video. Well, OK, yes, there's still a twitch, I grant. But it's minimal, surely? It can't be doing much damage. I'm getting a bit bored with all of this repetition, frankly.

Back home, I search the Internet. It turns out the human wrist can move in six ways – there's pronation and supination, dorsiflexion and palmarflexion and radial and ulnar deviation. Heck. So what about wrist rolling? Two hours, a medical dictionary and one hefty headache later, I conclude that the Knightsbridge crew believe golf is all about radial deviation – i.e., put your hand out as if about to shake hands with someone and cock the wrist upwards, with the thumb pointing towards your nose.

2.30 p.m.: I meet Dan, the Paxhill Park greenkeeper. Dan's thick-set and powerful and stomps about in ogre boots. There's something Heathcliffian about him. I picture him feasting on raw badger and living in underground caverns. He's the club champion, playing off three or four. He's self-taught and wins pretty much everything. He doesn't smile a lot, and talks even less. If he likes you, you might get a nod or a twitch of an eyebrow.

'How's it going?' I say.

He shrugs, looking like someone who's mislaid his favourite lawnmower.

'I'm getting bored with golf,' he growls.

He's just gone around Paxhill in a two-under-par 68, having hit every fairway and every green in regulation.

'I hit it straight, then I hit it on the green and putted out,' he complains, in a rare splurge of eloquence. 'Nothing really happened...'

'Yeah,' I reply as nonchalantly as possible. 'Know what you mean.'

The man's clearly an idiot. 68 boring? I'll give you boring. Boring's four lost balls per round. Boring's 24 over. You've been offered a glimpse of heaven on earth and found it boring? Men have killed for less.

2.45 p.m. I practise pointing my thumb at my nose.

3 p.m. Pick up Emma.

'What did you do at school?'

'Don't know. Can't remember. Nothing.'

Picks nose rebelliously. I press her. Apparently she's doing a dinosaur project.

'So what do herbivores eat?'

'Dinner,' she replies.

I'm left wondering whether six-year-olds do irony.

5 p.m. I've just realised – it's my birthday. That's what Post-Viral Fatigue does to you. My memory's got more holes in it than a slab of... of... of that Swiss cheese with holes in it.

It's a tedious illness. For most of the day, you look fine. There's no blood, stitches nor scars. All's hunky-dory. You're normal.

But gradually an opaque film seeps down over everything. When my eyes start to glaze – and I can sense it happening to the second – I'm on borrowed time. The colour drains from the day, my calf and thigh muscles ache as if I've just run a marathon and I feel someone's scooped out my bone marrow with a spoon. I'm tetchy and best out of the way.

The worst thing, though, isn't the fatigue. It's not even the bone marrow bit. It's that everybody you meet has heard of a miracle cure that helped their son, daughter, aunt, neighbour, MP, plumber, bridge partner or budgie.

It's invariably something wacky, involving cold baths, organic gluten-free blueberries from the Outer Hebrides and balancing upside down on your head while chanting Sanskrit. It's no use telling them you've already tried Chinese herbs, wheat-free diets, acupuncture, reflexology and aromatherapy. 'You must try this,' they insist. And often you do. And wish you hadn't bothered.

The other wretched thing is that your personality turns grey. You lose confidence and you're sapped of enthusiasm.

The good thing, though, is that I'm almost as good as new after an hour's nap. And it doesn't seem to affect me during golf rounds. I have yet to fall asleep during one.

Days 37–40: I have a cold bath, shop for gluten-free Outer Hebridean blueberries and continue with Pharro, Firkins, Lovell and Malins. They sound like a firm of solicitors. Public prosecutors, more like. I'm meant to be choosing between them but I feel my heels digging in.

Undeniable differences in style, language and emphasis emerge, but I don't see a problem. I revel in the variety of information on offer. Or perhaps, as usual, I just can't make up my mind.

Pharro and Firkins, in particular, hail from different planets. Pharro has a system and intends to crowbar me into it. He orders and demands. There's no discussion. That's a good thing, I think. I need a Sergeant Major in my life.

Firkins is less prescriptive and a lot more avuncular. He comes from a previous golfing age. He speaks softly and almost hesitantly. He suggests rather than dictates. He wants to build on what I've already got. Pharro thinks what I've got should be dynamited to the ground.

And while Pharro sleeps off his party hangovers on Sunday mornings, Firkins is in church.

It wasn't always like that. As a young man, Firkins worshipped golf. It was all he wanted. But he soon discovered that the life of an assistant club pro was less fulfilling than he'd envisaged. 'I used to clean hundreds of shoes and hundreds of golf clubs for the members every weekend. It was very hard work. I only got to play once a week.' He didn't much like the teaching, either.

Firkins kept true to his calling, though, and flirted with success. As a young man, he went down narrowly to future Open winner Bob Charles in the New Zealand matchplay. He qualified for the Open himself. There'd be a top-ten finish in the Portuguese Open. And he recorded wins over such Ryder Cup luminaries as Neil Coles, Ken Bousfield and George Will.

Firkins, though, prefers talking about others rather than himself.

'We've got two Ryder Cup players in the family, Bernard and Geoffrey Hunt – my cousins. And Bill Firkins, my father's brother, also qualified for the Ryder Cup. But the war broke out and he never played, unfortunately. My father was a fine player, too, a club champion. I played as a boy but I wasn't immediately good. I'm never immediately good at anything. I'm persistent.'

Firkins' route through life was diverted by 'a Damascus Road experience' when he was at Haywards Heath Golf Club. Until then, he'd sworn and blasphemed with the best of them. That stopped overnight when Firkins found God. 'It was a personal revelation and it was so powerful I could have given up golf there and then.'

For a few months, he barely played as he tried to come to terms with what had happened. 'I felt an inner directive telling me to go back to golf but to make sure that I kept it in perspective. From then on my game improved incredibly. I won more in the next ten years in Sussex and the southern region than I'd ever won before.'

Later, he'd split his time between golf and pastoral work for his church.

Today, he loves rather than resents teaching. 'It just shows how your life can change. I'm more patient. I try to keep things simple.'

Firkins follows a strict set-up routine, then focuses on relaxation, rhythm, fluidity and feel. 'I don't want you worrying about what your left arm or right leg are doing.'

He blames the hectic pace of modern life for high handicaps. 'I think techniques are generally better than they used to be, but people play less regularly.'

And the secret?

He laughs. 'You must realise you're always in submission to golf. It's always the master.'

I like Firkins. There's a wisdom to him. Sometimes I don't always understand what he means. Sometimes I feel he treats me too much like an adult and not enough as an idiot. But it invariably makes sense later. He's slow-burn. He's my antidote to Pharro.

So I try to fit everything each teacher says and mould it into a coherent whole. Crucially, they all agree about my wrists. Firkins also feels there's too much extraneous movement in my swing. He wants me to be more like Paul Casey. I want to be more like Paul Casey. He advocates a cut-fade to eliminate my smother-hook. For Malins, my hands are still too close to my thighs at address. He puts a glove under my left armpit to keep my takeaway together. He wants to cut out lateral sway. Lovell talks of coming into impact from the inside.

I begin, though, to overload. I 'pick and mix'. I delve into everything, I'm a Jack-of-all-trades while failing to master anything. I study magazine tips again, while reading Hogan's *Five Lessons*. I examine Byron Nelson's method and experiment with Sam Snead's ideas.

Things soon come to a head.

Day 45: I corner James at Paxhill.

'OK, OK,' he says, before I open my mouth. 'I can manage nine holes. Just nine.'

I'm in awe of James. He'd probably find the notion amusing. He can do everything I can't. He can chip out of heavy rough and fade his drives. He puts backspin on his pitches. He can mend buggies and stick clubheads back on.

I'm not surprised to hear that James is South African-born, Zimbabwe-bred. There's something of the Voortrekker about him. He's all self-reliance to my robin-reliance. He came to England as a student and never went back. After a successful career in information technology, he decided he deserved a change. He wound up his business dealings shortly after his fiftieth birthday and began making golf clubs. Without him, I reckon Paxhill would fall apart. Well, perhaps not quite. But the roof would fall in, the electrics blow, the heating pack up and there'd be abandoned buggies and headless clubs littering the place.

James has a nice take on club making.

'I'm selling joy,' he says. 'I can't guarantee to cut your handicap, or that you'll win more medals, but I can almost guarantee that you'll enjoy golf more. Properly fitted clubs should mean more good shots.'

We share the same philosophy. We both want to get better because we think hitting good shots is fun. When I've saved up enough, and I've improved enough, I'll talk to him in earnest about clubs. I see James as my on-course guide. I'm not sure how he sees me. As relatively harmless bacteria, probably.

'You ask a lot of questions,' he says. 'But you never remember the answers.'

Today James is going well and we play the whole eighteen. And, for the first time, I'm playing well too, relatively.

I'm hitting it more solidly. I feel my eclectic approach is paying off. I go through Firkins' set-up, I practise Pharro's takeaway, keeping the left wrist cupped, I tuck a fold of jumper under my left armpit (Malins). Eureka! My opening drive flies out between the bunkers to 240 yards!

I par the 1st hole for the very first time. I par the 2nd, for the very first time. I do the same on the 3rd. After five holes I'm 1 over. I've cracked it! I can play!

James brings me back down to earth. 'Keep it up,' he says. 'You look like a trussed chicken, but it seems to be working.'

And then, suddenly, my chickens become un-trussed and come home to roost. The sense of control vanishes. I've been cutting my drives and now they bank sharp left. I'm back to playing my second shots from the jungle. And I start beating myself up. It's an old, ingrained flaw. I start to make silent, sarcastic asides. 'Oh well played, Tony!' I hiss to myself after chunking the ball nowhere in particular. It's always been like this. It's as if I can hear the ghost of

Old Tom Morris, at his most acerbic, commentating on my disintegrating game.

On the 9th, I slice out of bounds. On the nasty par-three 12th I hook my three-wood into oblivion and slice the next into the adjoining field. I'm five off the tee and that's that.

In the bar, though, James is as complimentary as James gets. I've done well, he says. I've got around in 18 over – my best score. There've been a few pars and, unusually, a few successful putts. After two beers I revert to feeling hugely pleased with myself.

Day 47: Pharro is not pleased. Actually, he's hugely displeased. He asks to see a few more shots than usual, studies the video a little longer, then looks me in the eye.

'You've been sleeping around,' he says. 'You're seeing someone else.'

For a second, I feel like defending my position. 'Come on, Andy, surely you never imagined you were the only one? This was always an open relationship. We're both adults . . . '

Instead, rather less eloquently, I stammer: 'Er, well, hm, you see . . . '

What's given me away? My experiment of standing closer to the ball? Perhaps it was my dalliance with a fade? My attempt to copy Hogan's left wrist at impact or Nelson's leg action? Whatever it is, it stands out as clearly as crimson lipstick on white collars. Pharro can read the guilt all over my swing.

I come clean. There's Firkins, Lovell and Malins, there's the books, mags and videos. And I spend more time than is healthy watching The Golf Channel. But I'm intelligent enough, I maintain, to make sense of it all.

'No,' says Pharro, 'you're not. It won't work. You're

messing about with everything and you haven't even sorted out your takeaway.'

The rest of the lesson takes place five degrees on the far side of frosty.

'If Mr King had been in charge and you'd consulted other teachers,' Pharro concludes, 'you wouldn't have been invited back.'

Returning home, I think things over. I've been caught 'in flagrante'. But it begs the question – who's in charge of whom? The good thing, I suppose, is that Pharro got angry. It suggests he cares. But where do I go from here?

Day 55: The doorbell rings. I'm painting the loft. Under strict orders, I've sacrificed this week's golf to dabble in Dulux. So the doorbell rings and that can mean only one thing – human interaction.

That's the trouble with house husbandry. Companionship is in short supply. There's the VSPMs and LBAALMFPMs (Laid Back And A Lot More Fun Playground Mums), of course, and Geraldine and Jemima (Emma's gerbils). But it's still a life within narrow walls.

I filter dutifully through the dirty washing and burnt saucepans but fail to uncover a single anecdote to share with Jan. I don't envy her the daily commute, but I envy the emotions involved, even if they include anger and frustration. At least she's alive, even if she never gets a seat on the train. It's hard to be emotional while cleaning the toilet bowl. I've stopped reading newspapers and, on bad days, watch daytime television. I wince, but it's true – I know the names of all the *Big Brother* contestants.

So the bell rings and I leap off the ladder and down the first flight of stairs and across the landing and down again. I'm nearly there and I'm sure they won't have gone yet, I'll speak to anybody, Frank next door, Nicky from across the road, the postman, the greengrocer, God, I'll even invite Jehovah's Witnesses in for a cup of tea if they've got the time . . .

And then I trip. My left foot skids over the edge of a step and I land on my toe ends and there's a distinct crack. It must be the floorboards. I scream out a few choice, colourful oaths, compose myself, hop-scotch to the door and open it to see two Jehovah's Witnesses beetling towards the end of the drive in panic, fingers in their ears.

By the time I've removed my sock two toes are already going a nasty colour. Within half an hour they're black and no longer fit into my shoe. By evening I'm limping out of the doctor's surgery in possession of a double fracture and a pocketful of aspirin.

A day or two later, I catch the 'flu. Not men's 'flu. The real stuff. And then the rain begins to fall. Not men's rain. The real stuff. Non-stop and heavy. I won't be playing golf for a while.

EIGHT

TRABANTS AND MERCEDES

'Do you wish to rise? Begin by descending. You plan a tower that will pierce the clouds? Lay first the foundation of humility'

— Saint Augustin

Weight: 13st 2lb
Waist measurement: Twiggy-like. Circa 36–37in. Trousers falling off.
Diet: Lemsips, aspirin, Emma's Calpol.
Alcohol: Zero.
Chronic Fatigue: Too sleepy to calculate.
Official handicap: 24
Rounds: 6
Average score per round: 24 over
Eagles: 0
Longest drive: 240 yards (14 November, Paxhill, 1st)
Number of range balls hit: 1,150
Self-belief: 4/10
And the secret of golf is . . . Hugh Grant, possibly.

1 December: Day 63, 302 to go.

8.15 a.m. I practise pointing my thumb at my nose but miss.

Emma discusses her school project over breakfast. 'It's about a boat called *The Titanic*,' she declares, her face in the Rice Krispies. 'It got sunk by an ice cube.'

9 a.m. Back after drop-off. Foot propped up on a chair. Now

let's be positive. Things could be worse. It could be gorgeous golfing weather, instead of incessant rain. I'm not the only one being deprived.

Let's recap. I'm two months in. What have I achieved?

Well, on the downside, I've been 'sacked' by my teacher. The major plus, though, is that I've cut four shots – unofficially – off my handicap. Mind you, I lost those in the very first week. And teeing off with a six-iron instead of a driver feels like a cop-out. I've also lost 8lb in weight, although that was 'flu. I've played six rounds and hit more than 1,000 range balls. My wrists still roll. I'm more confused than ever. I'd hoped to find this easier. At times I feel like chucking it in.

So far so bad. So what am I going to do over the next two weeks, apart from hobble about with a paintbrush? I scrutinise my navel.

9.06 a.m. Let's go and scrutinise someone else's navel. Let's have a coffee at Burgess Hill range.

I'm not quite sure what I have in mind. For starters, I don't drink coffee. I have about six hours of energy available per day, to be rationed over the fourteen hours between Emma-rise and Emma-set. One cup of coffee, I estimate, offers a heart-thudding forty-five-minute high while confiscating two hours of my daily fuel. But sod it, so what? Let's live a little. I sit down at the back of the range and daydream.

Lovell comes up to say hello and goodbye. He's moving to a new job. So now I'm two teachers down.

An hour passes. Then another. One cup of coffee becomes two, then three. Golfers of all shapes and sizes wander in and out.

At first I stare aimlessly. Then I begin to look. Then I begin to see. I've come out for caffeine, fresh air and a moment of reflection. What I get is an education. I discover how not to do things. In essence, I'm watching myself.

My first impression is that most golfers hit a lot of balls, and they hit them fast. There's no suggestion of pre-shot routines, nor finishes being held. People thrash as if they have trains to catch. They smash and grab. There are far, far more bad shots than good ones, accompanied by loud complaints about the unfairness of the game in particular and of life in general. There seems to be a universal presumption that, because the odd ball flies straight, the rest are duty-bound to follow suit. No one considers that the straight one might have been a fluke.

Some start hitting in more measured fashion but inevitably speed up. Many come with the intention of buying one bucket – particularly the be-suited businessmen – but end up squeezing in an extra two or three. Their lunch breaks turn into a golf-ball feeding frenzy.

The other striking thing is how easy most errors are to identify. I'm not suggesting I know how to fix them. But there are a lot of funny grips. Wasn't it Sam Snead who said that if most people gripped their knives and forks like their golf clubs they'd starve to death? Some people aim left at set-up and some right. Some come over the top and others collapse their arms. Some sway and tilt rather than turn. Some stand bolt upright, others bend double, nose to kneecaps. None of the perpetrators seems to suspect what they're perpetrating. One-eyed, they gaze into fairground mirrors and see Tiger Woods smiling back.

There's a tragic inevitability to the process. Man addresses ball. Man swipes. Ball skims 30 yards along ground. Man utters expletive before apologising to neighbours. Man addresses ball. Identical swipe. Identical result. Identical expletive. Man addresses ball . . . It's a perfect demonstration of Albert Einstein's definition of insanity: 'Doing the same thing over and over again and expecting different results.'

And everyone shows a reckless disregard for the basics. Perhaps they've forgotten them. Or perhaps – and I put my own hand up here – they think that basics are for beginners. 'Grip? Posture? Balance? Weight transfer? Gosh, no! I'm working on something much more complicated . . .'

I get a flashback. I'm spending the summer with my friend Tilman and his family near Stuttgart while trying half-heartedly to improve my German before university. Tilman is forever larking about but always, he maintains, in the name of science. One day he wonders if drugs work on dogs. He duly blows cannabis smoke up his sedentary boxer's nostrils. Boris the boxer seems keen to find out too. He does a lot of licking. The experiment ends with him – Boris, not Tilman – hurtling at high speed three times round the house before keeling over, legs in the air, and falling fast asleep.

Tilman's major project that summer, though, is to transplant a West German Mercedes engine into an East German Trabant.

Trabants weren't really cars. They were fibreglass egg boxes, powered by rubber bands, pedals and party propaganda. As a symbol of Communism's technological sophistication, they lacked conviction. They could reputedly hit top speeds of about 90mph, but only when travelling down the north face of the Eiger with a following gale. Tilman had purchased a vomit-green model with the intention of souping up its performance. The idea was to draw up alongside the latest Porsche on the autobahn and give a dismissive, regal wave before accelerating away in a cloud of smoke and a swath of acrid, burning rubber.

So he dismantled his dad's second Mercedes – I never did discover whether Tilman senior was a consenting party – widened the Trabant chassis, removed the rear seats and remodelled the engine. The result? Well, he took it for a test drive on a disused airfield and things went perfectly at first. But by the time the Trabant had hit 135mph, a high-pitched grinding sound began and thick oily smoke engulfed the car. As Tilman slowed to assess the damage, the rear axle sheared in two, the Trabant hit the Tarmac in a burst of sparks and disintegrated into 10,000 shards. Tilman didn't stop laughing for a week.

That's what I'm reliving now at Burgess Hill range – golfers with Mercedes ambitions, welded on to Trabant sub-frames. No wonder the wheels are falling off.

Watching Burgess Hill lessons is equally instructive. There aren't too many. Most golfers have no intention of wasting money on tuition. Everyone knows that there are plenty of free tips in magazines. Or just ask a mate along, some fellow 20-handicapper with plenty of opinions. He'll surely chip in with something useful.

The case for Do-It-Yourself golf seems suddenly half-baked to me. It's hardly surprising. We all know someone with a passion for domestic DIY. They're the ones whose houses are falling down. As for those who do take lessons, well, the majority aren't too susceptible to new ideas.

One rotund gentleman rolls up in a Jaguar, sporting a Rolex and bristling with new Pings. I'm not convinced he's wearing his own hair. His swing looks inside out and back to front but when the pro starts to realign him he protests: 'Hey, hey, I don't want to be messed about with here . . . '

There's an imposing woman who won't let her teacher get a word in edgeways. I hear later she's a local magistrate. 'I know what I'm doing wrong,' she announces as a way of introduction, peering at the twenty-two-year-old assistant pro over her pince-nez as though he should be in Borstal.

Then there's the young, thrusting bank manager due to play with his boss next week. He's exaggerated. He's told his boss he's a golfer, figuring it can't be so very difficult. So he wants a passable golf game from his teacher. Within, say, the next thirty minutes.

Others want to discuss golf's latest best-seller, expounding the virtues of a new, revolutionary, guaranteed-or-your-money-back golf gadget. Or a groundbreaking DVD containing earth-shattering new theories that look set to transform the sport (with a bonus head cover and twelve max-distance balls thrown in for free).

'Teach me that,' they demand.

And why not? It's perfectly understandable to want to be transformed into a golfer immediately rather than waste months practising. I'd like that, too. What's so wrong with believing in magic, miracles, fairies and elves? Emma does (although she's having doubts about Father Christmas – she can't fathom how he visits all the world's children in a single night when it takes us almost as long to drive around the M25 to Granny's).

I limp back to the car. It's been entertaining but I have to get back home. The coffee's last kick is wearing off. A coma threatens.

When I wake up on the lounge sofa two hours later I'm still buzzing. I'm still not sure I've answered one of my central questions – who is to blame for Man In The Street's golfing ineptitude, teacher or student? – but it seems criticism can be levelled at both.

I feel I've learnt another thing. Golf ranges are responsible for wrecking more swings than they fix.

I pick up my clubs with a new sense of purpose and practise my takeaway while balancing on my eight good toes. I'll make my peace with Pharro. I'll stick to his basics-first policy. I'll return to Knightsbridge and plead that it's all my fault. I'll practise whatever he preaches, for however long it takes. I'll curb the temptation to over-complicate. I'll sack Firkins and Malins. I'll bonfire my golf magazines, videos and instructional aids.

And I'll do what I always intended – I'll write out a specific programme to improve in all areas, not just the long game. I'll recruit a variety of gurus and sages to help me learn how to putt, chip and pitch. I'll do sit-ups and I'll look into the mental game. I'll eat better, drink less and weigh less. I'll get serious. On one hour a day.

Day 65: I'm Googling.

'Putting expert', I type. I am offered 2,640,000 options. Jeez. What about 'putting expert Haywards Heath'? Hm, better. Only 10,700.

On a whim, I try 'Population Haywards Heath'. Apparently there are 22,800 inhabitants of my home town. Amazing. Almost half are covert putting experts! I had no idea. Statistically, there should be one in our house, but that can't be, surely? It's certainly not me, and I don't think it's Emma. I've never seen Jan putt, come to think of it.

It turns out there's a guy called Jason Gilroy near by. Perhaps I should give him a call? But I'm on a roll. I type in 'golf fitness' – 7,590,000 possibilities. Then 'golf psychologist' – 218,000. There are even 176,000 hypnotists who'll benefit your game. That's a truly appealing concept – improving while taking a nap.

The most eye-opening search, however, comes when I write 'golf secret'. I had hoped for a single offer. But there are almost 12,000,000 people out there willing and able to reveal their secret to you. At a price.

Day 66: It's raining again. My toes turn from blue to yellow. I feel a bit low. I blame Frank next door.

Frank and I, as fellow 'working-from-home-occasionally' types, used to share morning and afternoon cups of tea. Recently, though, he's been avoiding me. He has a point. I do rather go on about golf. Actually, I do rather go on and on. And on. I've turned into an obsessive since September, a serial one-trick pony, and it's got worse since my toe break. Call it a character flaw, but I find it extraordinary that anybody could not be as interested in my multiple swing theories as I am.

Frank will try anything to change the subject but I'm a rabid dog with a bone.

'My father died recently,' Frank said the other day, after I called by to pontificate on the value of a smooth downswing.

He wasn't lying, exactly. It depends on your definition of the word 'recently'. To some people that could mean a few days. To Frank, it meant eight years.

I responded correctly enough.

'I'm very sorry to hear that, Frank,' I replied, and bowed my head in respectful contemplation.

I felt 4.82 seconds of silence was appropriate.

'Did he play golf at all?'

Now Frank pretends he's not home. He impersonated an

answer phone the other day. So I went round. I spotted him reading a book in the lounge when I walked up to the front door, but no one came when I rang the bell. I peered through the front window, my hands cupped around my eyes, and rapped on the glass but Frank seemed to have vanished.

I go to the club. Paxhill is deserted. Out on the course, all I can see are saturated temporary greens and the odd Vet trapped up to his waist in quicksand. Apparently someone is trying to buy the club, which I find hard to believe. A rice farmer, probably. I spot James and start talking. He raises his arms in surrender.

Day 73: I bite the bullet and head for Knightsbridge. I meet Gould.

'Has Hugh Grant been in?' I ask. 'I wanted a chat.'

'He was here. You just missed him. So was Christopher Lee. And D.J. Spoony. And . . . '

Damn and blast.

'What about Dave?'

'He was here a minute ago too,' replies Gould, whirling his arms wildly about in the air, one clockwise and the other anti-clockwise, for no apparent reason. 'Where can he have got to?'

Pharro smooths in, smiling. 'Ah, Lord Antony! I wasn't sure you'd be back.'

He videos my swing and an odd thing happens. Pharro is vaguely complimentary. Very, very vaguely.

'Not perfect, not great, but not bad,' he says. 'Not . . . too . . . bad.'

I rush over to the monitor, in a state of excitement. But no. There is still a noticeable wrist flick, and my left arm still detaches from my body. As bad as ever.

'No,' says Pharro. 'Really, it's better. Yes, you still roll a bit, at the start and as you approach the horizontal, but you're halfway there to getting the first 2 feet of the takeaway. We'll go a bit further next time.'

Day 76: Jan doesn't know it, but I'm testing her. I'm measuring the strength of our relationship – on a scale of one to five – by leaving golf clubs all around the house. Jan doesn't like clutter. One club left out without her demanding it put away equals nostalgic affection. Two equals friendship. Three, solid commitment. Four, true love. Five, utter besottedness.

So far, I've proved true love. Besottedness is not out of the question, either – I've yet to risk leaving out a wood. Mind you, I concede that the exact opposite may be true. Jan may have become so indifferent that she wouldn't notice if I switched channels in the middle of a lavish BBC period costume drama in favour of a goal-less stalemate between two Belgian third division football sides.

To be honest, it didn't begin as a test. It began as laziness. I began sneaking out my eight-iron to practise my grip, takeaway or full swing while eating crisps in the living room. One day, I left the club concealed behind the lamp. When Jan did not complain, it became a fixture. Then I slipped my seven-iron next to the bookcase in the dining room – there's more room to swing there, and you can see your reflection in the French windows.

The pitching-wedge followed in the kitchen, propped up in the vegetable box next to the fridge. Still no complaints. Remarkable, for a woman who puts the ironing board back in the cupboard while I'm in the middle of shirt collars. Now I'm even taking full swings without prompting protest. She's not only in earshot, she can even see me. I'm getting away with murder. Our relationship is as sound as a bell.

Mind you, there's still that nagging doubt.

I flick through the TV guide. *Sense and Sensibility* is on (again) tonight. And Racing Club Mechelen, just by chance, are away at R.A.E.C. Mons on one of the lesser sports channels.

Day 82: 5.15 a.m. I steal from the house, armed with clubs, shoes, a litre water bottle, a sports drink, two bananas, an energy bar, an apple and a bag of nuts. I'm as excited as Emma is about the 1,750 presents bearing her name under the Christmas tree. A friend has invited me to play at Goodwood, just north of Chichester. I've barely played for a month. I snatched a round at Paxhill three days ago and went round in a phenomenal 17 over. Best of all, I had always promised myself that I'd return my woods to my bag once I scored under 18 over. So I'm fully, lethally equipped again.

I plan for an hour's warm-up. Niall, a fellow journalist-turned-author, will probably turn up ten minutes late. Life does not get much better than this. Goodwood is a seriously good course. I hope not to make a complete arse of myself. There's nothing on the roads apart from me and a few compressed foxes. I get to the club one hour, forty-five minutes ahead of schedule. It's freezing, pitch-black and there are no lights on. I drive around to Niall's home in the hope of a bacon sandwich but it's still in darkness. I return to the club and practise my swing in the car park while trying desperately to warm up.

Niall eventually dawdles up, under a shag of unruly hair and carrying a golf set which last saw action in the Crimean War. There's a thick frost underfoot and the ground is as unyielding as iron. Nothing, though, can spoil the day.

Niall played as a teenager. People who played as kids, in my experience, are invariably better than they admit. Niall tells me he is the worst golfer in southern England. He used to play only a couple of weeks per year, he maintains, accompanied by his brother, a six-pack of lager and half a bottle of whisky.

I expect Padraig Harrington. Niall's first strike scuttles 130 yards into a ditch. I feel better immediately. As the worst two golfers in southern England, we should be evenly matched.

I struggle on the snooker-table greens. At the 5th, I chip onto the green only to discover that the front fringe dips sharply off to the right. My ball rolls down into a deep valley. The valley's full of divot marks, snapped wedges and human remains. I chip back on, overcook the putt coming back and the ball rolls back into the valley.

There are successes, though. The final hole is a daunting 400-yard par four. I hit the longest drive of my life, 245 yards through a collection of bunkers, then connect so well with my six-iron that I go 20 feet past. I go round in 24 over. Niall stops counting after thirty.

We ruminate over a beer. I've just realised how much golf courses can differ. My 17 over at Paxhill felt no better than my 24 over at Goodwood. So do I play to 17 or am I a 24? I'll ask James.

Home, I empty my bag of the untouched litre water bottle, sports drink, two bananas, energy bar, apple and bag of nuts.

Day 86: Christmas Eve. The Wurzels — Jan's parents Ken and Marianne and her brother John — are visiting, along with their collection of interminable stories about fish that got away, about otters, red squirrels, woodpeckers, peregrines, wood-lice, grubs and other such fascinating creatures. It's like being force-fed Gerald Durrell.

I listen as best I can while trying not to doze off. I went close to killing most of Jan's family in a car crash in France once, so I owe them some licence. My mother-in-law proved her mettle that day. Tough old bird. She kept talking in her broad Somerset, saying everything was just fine and dandy, as they stitched up her battered lip and bloody leg. The French surgeons smiled, not understanding a syllable. Ken broke his back and needed a major operation in Bordeaux. Jan didn't get off much better. That was fifteen years ago. But every now and again, normally when I'm driving, I wince at the memory.

Anyway, each to his own. I prefer my own tall tales, about the putts which lipped out and the drives that deserved so much more. I sneak out early in the morning again, for Paxhill. It's crisp, cold and still. With nobody to be seen, I head out through the mist and on to the course.

I give pitching a go.

I never have a clue what club to take, or how hard to swing, whenever I get to within 100 yards. So I measure out distances of 90, 80, 70, 60 and 50 paces and spend forty-five blissful minutes practising. I'm not sure I learn much but I enjoy the space.

I'm all but fifty, and all but unemployed. I am about to celebrate my first adult Christmas without a job. I've lost sight of all the measures and yardsticks that used to chart my life. The only thing that now defines me is the school run, bad cooking and questionable golf. I don't feel particularly valuable.

Walking down the 18th, I spot a deer grazing. It looks up and stares, momentarily concerned, then drops its head gracefully and continues feeding for a few carefree minutes. I decide not to mention the deer to The Wurzels.

NINE

A PENNY DROPS

'Be precise. A lack of precision is dangerous when the margin of error is small'

— Donald Rumsfeld

Weight: 13st 4lb
Waist measurement: 37in – no increase over Christmas.
Diet: Peculiarly sensible since festivities.
Alcohol: Peculiarly extravagant during festivities (to counter Wurzel waffle).
Chronic Fatigue: Improving, I think. I hope.
Official handicap: 24
Rounds: 7
Average score per round: 22.85 over
Eagles: 0
Longest drive: 245 yards (21 December, Goodwood, 18th hole).
Range balls: 1,400
Self-belief: 5/10
And the secret of golf is . . . avoid driving ranges.

Day 94, 271 to go. New Year.
Emma's not speaking to me. She left me in charge of her Christmas Tamagotchi (a handheld digital pet, since you ask) last night but this morning it was dead. Apparently I didn't feed it enough hamburgers or ice creams or something. How was I supposed to know? Ridiculous present! I mean, what sort of diet is that? Well, fairly familiar, if I'm honest . . .

I write my New Year's Resolutions list. The one I write every year.

1) Learn Spanish.
2) Learn to play guitar and/or piano and/or rest of orchestra.
3) Read Proust's *À la recherche du temps perdu* in the original.
4) Lose weight/get fitter/no more biscuits.
5) Take up yoga.
6) Be a better person/be nice to animals (excluding Tom, the one-eyed cat who defecates in our garden).
7) Give up Spanish after two weeks.
8) eBay the guitar for half price.
9) Don't read Proust in the original (or in English, for that matter).
10) Gain weight . . .

I'm casting too wide, as usual. Try again. Stick to basics.

1) Play one/two rounds of golf in single figures by the end of September.
2) Beat my brothers in one round of strokeplay.
3) Be more patient with Emma (up to a point).
4) Cook better (edibly).
5) Increase golf practice to ninety minutes a day.
6) Improve health/lose weight. Less biscuits/alcohol. More water/veg.
7) Question experts about handicaps and the secret of golf.
8) Stop shaving until I score in single figures.

I don't get to a tenth resolution for the first time in years. It's a relief not to have to pretend to be learning Spanish and the guitar.

Day 97: Paxhill. Sleet and slushy snow. The course is a quagmire. In the bar, a motley crew recall great shots they imagine once playing, each narrator trumping his neighbour.

'No, no,' shouts Tweedle Dum, 'it was 295 yards. Into a two-club wind. And uphill, definitely uphill . . . '

They sound like my brother-in-law and his sprats-cum-great-whites. They chew the cud from the depths of their armchairs. They talk golf shots, and football teams, and cars and jobs, but reveal nothing. Nothing personal, anyway. It's all about ritual. The rituals of blokes all together. I've never been much good at it.

I risk the range. I'm coming over the top. My divots point left. The other day I was slicing, now I'm pulling. I return home despondent. I don't dare ask Pharro. He doesn't think I'm hitting balls yet. Towards midnight, I fire up the computer and Google 'golf swing transition'. 103,000 options.

I read most of them before dawn. Apparently I've got to keep my back to the target for a second longer while moving my left knee down the line and shifting my hips laterally, then rotationally, which in turn will drop my arms, with wrists still cocked, into the correct slot and make me squat powerfully, thus increasing torque before I fire through with my right side while, of course, keeping my head behind the ball and retaining my spine angle.

Or words to that effect. Right. At least that's been cleared up.

Day 99: 13st 5lb. The scales must be faulty. Swing my six-iron in front of the living room mirror but give up after catching the side of the sofa. Use a bit of spit and shoe polish to hide the damage. Jan'll never know. Promise myself to do sit-ups tomorrow. Three glasses of wine.

Day 100: 13st 7lb. It's absurd! Where the heck did those two extra pounds come from? I barely ate a thing yesterday. And I barely moved! How do you gain weight by not moving? I devour a packet of salt and vinegar in frustration. Swing my seven-iron but hurt my back. Am I overdoing it? Put off sit-ups. Three glasses of wine but also drink a glass of water and eat a portion of raw vegetables. To make up for the crisps.

Day 101: Rest day. Do not weigh myself. Or rather, start to but then jump off as the needle passes 13st 7lb. Buy two golf magazines but do not get round to reading them. Four glasses of wine.

Day 104: Brother Martin emails to suggest a game at Burhill. I'm not sure, post Goodwood, that I'm ready for another testing course. And I'd rather take on my brothers at the end of the year. This is too early. But it'll be a lovely day and Martin will pay for everything – he always does – so at least I'll be able to be envious of his house, cars, golf clubs, holiday plans and entire life while speed-drinking as much free Guinness as possible.

Actually, you can't be jealous of Martin. He's a good sort. He's always worked his socks off for his millions. Good luck to him.

Actually, on reflection, I think you can quite easily be jealous of the rich bastard.

I say yes, if only for the Guinness.

By way of preparation for Martin I head to Paxhill for nine holes with James.

'You need a shave,' he says.

My left-leaning divots continue to defy my best endeavours but I hit the ball nicely enough and scramble around in seven over. Blimey – that would be 14 over if I'd kept going! I chip uncharacteristically nicely.

I tell James about Goodwood, and how hard I found the course. He tells me about 'course rating' and 'slope rating'. Apparently it's some sort of system used to help calculate handicaps while also taking into account the relative difficulty of golf courses. I'm a bit blinded by the science but I get the general point. Paxhill is regarded as easy, Goodwood isn't. A 24-handicapper at Goodwood would thus be, say, as good as a 20-handicapper at Paxhill.

I decide, for the sake of accurate comparison, to retain only my scorecards from Paxhill and Poult Wood. They're about the same standard.

Day 107: Now I know this sounds absurd but it must be said – I've never seen the point of putting.

I get soaring drives from elevated tees, and mid-irons fired across lakes on to tree-lined greens. They're marvellous captions to perfect pictures. They're poetry. They're joy. They make your day.

Putts break your day. Even good putts are expressions of relief, prosaic full stops calling a halt to the poetry. Fine, fine, they're necessary. 'They count as much as a 300-yard drive,' I hear you say. Sure. Right. But whoever got excited composing a full stop?

Niall phoned the other day to say he's driven one of Goodwood's shorter par fours. 'I belted it 300 yards, dead straight,' he enthused. Better still, the threesome ahead lingered long enough to witness his miracle shot and broke out into spontaneous applause.

'They moved off, I marched on to the green . . . and four-putted.'

That sums up putting. A carbuncle on a near-perfect sport.

Look what happened to that nice Mr Langer. A good Christian, a good father and husband, he was afflicted by the yips for years. Fate, of course, decreed that the deciding putt of the 1991 Ryder Cup at Kiawah Island should fall to him. Downright cruel, I call it. I still remember Bernard's contorted face as his 6-footer slid past.

And what about Doug Sanders on the 18th at St Andrews in 1970? That one was a 3-footer, but the American jabbed at it with all the composure of a man shaking hands with a rattlesnake. He missed, then lost the play-off to Jack Nicklaus. Sanders came second in four majors but never won one. At least he didn't let it affect him. Asked, years later, if that miss still haunted him, he replied: 'No. Some days I can go twenty minutes without thinking about it.'

I think putting should be banned. They call it a game within a game. I'd like to make it a game without a game. Some people have tried to do just that. It's called 'crazy golf'. It attracts sad congregations of eccentrics who converge on faded, weather-beaten seaside resorts and putt at concrete tunnels, mini waterfalls and Don Quixote windmills.

Some say putting reflects depth of character. I'm not so sure. I don't think I'm more fragile than my brothers but they're forever making putts from 10 to 20 feet while making me hole out from 10 to 20 inches. A 'gimmee', it is said, is an agreement between two individuals, neither of whom putt well. Quite sensibly, I confess, nobody ever gives me anything.

Matthew once told me I'd have to fall in love with putting before improving as a golfer. I ignored him but he was right.

If I don't get the point of putting, I'm hardly going to get the point of 'putting expert' Jason Gilroy.

As I drive to his West Sussex base, I picture a man in a 1970s tank top with unfashionably thick bi-focals. When not drooling over his Scotty Camerons and C-groove putters, I picture Gilroy on a windswept railway platform, scribbling down numbers. He'll probably have a tell-tale tick, some urgent, metronomic nod of the head or involuntary spasm. Putting does that to you. If it doesn't make you go quite mad it will at least scar your soul.

He opens the door. There's no sign of a tank top. He looks unsettlingly normal. He's clearly in disguise.

I introduce myself: 'Hi. I'm Tony. I'm the world's worst putter.'

He laughs. I don't.

Gilroy's studio bristles with hi-tech gadgetry. There's a laser beam lining you up to the hole and ultrasound sensors on your putter shaft, relaying a battery of information on to a wall-mounted screen. You stand on thermographic 'force plates' to highlight any shifts in balance during the stroke. And there's the inevitable video, in case you do not feel humiliated enough already.

I feel like a lab rat contemplating its own dissection.

'The system can measure twenty-eight parameters in all,' says Gilroy. 'The main ones are aim, face and path direction, impact spot, loft and rise angles, rotation and timing and rhythm. It's accurate to 0.1 of a degree.'

Gilroy adores putting. He also admits to being 'a bit of a techno freak'.

The SAM Puttlab (Science And Motion, not Surface-to-Air Missile) was developed by two German doctors. Their original intent was to use ultrasound sensors to study how neurological processes related to the control of the body. They soon realised, though, that the technology had other applications.

'Most people don't take enough care of their putting,' adds Gilroy. 'The short game's the area they should be working hardest on. The pros do. Talk to them after a round and they invariably remember putts rather than drives.'

Gilroy played county golf as a youngster. After a spell in the Armed Forces, he visited Tour School and played on the Sunshine Tour in South Africa, winning a qualifier. He also had a bite at the Challenge Tour. Without instant success, however, you need deep pockets – or generous benefactors – to survive long.

He supplemented his earnings by teaching.

'I taught the full swing but I had a much greater passion for putting. The idea of specialising had been bubbling away for years. I'd always been a good putter. I was known as "Up-and-Down Bill from Brazil". Get me to 10 feet and I'm confident I can hole out. It's just one of those things. I've never really had a formal lesson.'

Now he's got me to deal with – 'Three-putt Pete from Paxhill Park'. I'm not sure what to expect. I come as a blank sheet of paper. I can discuss long-game theory late into the night but putting's a mystery. I've no idea why I'm so poor. Is it, as Matthew says, down to lack of interest? Do I stand too close to the ball? Am I too wristy? No idea. It's hard to have a philosophy when you haven't got a clue.

I've often left playing partners bemused by my incompetence.

I remember one round with Paul the Builder. Paul built our loft extension. Paul thumps the ball agriculturally. I went round in 17 over to his 23, but on the greens there was only one winner. Paul's Schwarzenegger became Michelangelo.

'This one breaks to the right at first but there's a flat bit in the middle and then it turns the other way,' he'd say.

All I could see was a patch of closely mown grass. It didn't matter what I did. I could plumb-bob or lie down on my stomach, nose to the ground. It was still just a patch of grass.

'Didn't you spot the break?' he'd ask, perplexed, as I missed yet another 4-footer.

'No, I bloody well didn't,' I snarled. 'And I still don't.'

Afterwards, Paul explained that he could look at a 20ft roof beam and sense whether it was an inch off the horizontal without resorting to a spirit level. That explained his ability. It didn't begin to make sense of my dyslexia.

Gilroy asks me to take five 15-foot putts. My aim is reasonable enough, he says, and my putter path not too bad. My grip gets tweaked – it's too much like my ordinary golf grip. Then Gilroy shows me a graph of squiggly coloured lines on the screen.

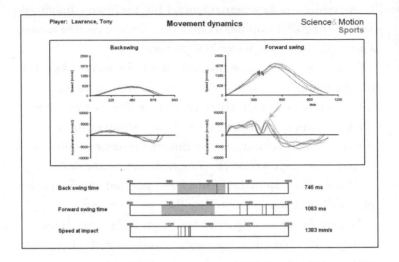

'You're accelerating your putter head after impact,' he says.

I'm accelerating my putter AFTER impact? That's absurd. Why would anybody do that? It makes no sense at all.

Apparently, though, it's quite common. The coloured lines, depicting clubhead motion, reveal that my putter starts back at a decent speed, loses impetus, then picks up pace after the strike.

'You decelerate, then try to salvage things when it's already too late. A bit like putting at fresh air. Basically, you've got a long, woolly stroke. You're going back too far and coming in too slowly. It's indecisive.'

Another five putts and I'm just as squiggly. Gilroy demonstrates. And I experience a revelation. Putting really can be beautiful!

I learn a lot more. For starters, there's no one method. Some people take the putter head inside-to-inside, others square-to-square. Some opt for forward presses. Some hit down, others up.

'I advise a few key fundamentals but there are almost as many putting philosophies as there are ways to swing a club,' Gilroy says. 'It's your personal fingerprint.'

He discusses American pro Billy Mayfair's 'cut stroke'. It's not one you'd teach but it's been good enough to win $20 million or so. Mayfair tried to change his putting once, following 'expert' criticism. Result? He stopped winning. So he reverted and the dollars came pouring in again.

'And look at Nicklaus. He hunched over, with everything open to the line apart from his forearms and shoulders. It didn't do him any harm.'

We discuss psychology, and how golfers tie themselves in mental knots. Many professionals have hundreds of putters cluttering up their garages.

'Some people can't stop themselves. They get a new putter and things are great for a two-week honeymoon and then the process starts all over again.'

Anyone can have a bad day, of course. Even Gilroy.

'I had three guests with me at a pro-am. The 1st hole was a long par three and I reached the fringe with an OK three-iron. I'd just come from the office, with 101 things burning in my head. I had a putt of about 40 feet and got to within 10, with a little right-to-left break. No problem. But I missed it and it went 4 feet past. Then I missed that one. Then I missed the next. The worst thing was that I'd already introduced myself as a putting specialist.

'I felt like walking off the course there and then. Instead I ripped up my business card and threw it in the bin. And what happened? I went on to hole absolutely everything and shot 5 under. It had just been a matter of clearing my mind. A couple of my playing partners that day booked up for lessons.'

Gilroy keeps returning to one point.

'The mechanics are the underlying factor,' he says. 'I've no doubt that working on your mechanics will solve your problems. I'm certain we can take three or four shots off your score. I've taught people averaging forty-plus putts a round. Some read too many books. Some opt for DIY. Either way, they don't really understand what's going on. You want to improve. Many golfers never make that decision.'

I leave with a computer disk detailing my failings. As I drive home, I try to remember them — long woolly stroke, accelerating after impact, too strong a grip. But the thing that remains with me has nothing to do with my inadequacies. It's the image of Gilroy putting. His stroke is compact, rhythmical and unhurried. His putter head glides. And the ball ends up in the hole an awful lot.

I search for the right description. There and then the penny drops.

'Precision . . . that's it!' I say to myself. 'His stroke is surgically precise.'

His putting stroke carbon-copies itself, again and again. That precision can only come, I figure, from precise, repetitive practice. All I have to do now is emulate him. I must bore myself to death.

Another thought strikes me. Surely it would be good to transfer that precision to my long game? Golf is not like football, where you can mis-kick continuously but still be the hero with a ninetieth-minute winner, or cricket, where you concede fifty runs off five overs, drop three catches, run out your captain but then hook a match-winning six off the final ball of the match.

In golf, you get no credit for bloody-minded effort or courage.

Every stroke is marked down in the debit column. Every one counts. You can't have it back. Miss your chosen dimple by half an inch and you miss the green by a mile. It's a sport for marksmen, for cool, quiet men. I'm a verbose hot head, bouncing up and down on a trampoline with a blunderbuss.

2 p.m. I go for an afternoon nap but wake up feeling somebody else's age. I get the overwhelming feeling that I'm no longer young. I want to be a twenty-year-old again, focused and exact, 11st 7lb and with a 30-inch waist. Somehow, somewhere along the road, I've become a middle-aged doormat.

But the moment passes. I've got Emma to pick up, and her school friend Sarah (or is it Tarin this time?) as well, and there isn't a single fish finger in the house, nor carrots, ice cream or maple syrup. I could have a two-girl riot on my hands. And with that, any further golfing thoughts slip out of my mind.

Day 112: My chin itches. I'm not sure I like beards.

Today I'm going putting with Firkins and Malins.

I never did get round to sacking them. I'm not sure I ever intended to. Look, they add perspective. They offer differing viewpoints. I must just make sure I don't mix their ideas with Pharro's. If they champion conflicting methods, I'll just stop listening.

Let's be clear. Firkins is no mug. He may not be as fashionable or as hirsute as Pharro – who is? – but he's played at the top level. As for Malins, he's playing county events. He's fun and enthusiastic and hits the ball over mountains.

If there's a problem it's me, not them.

Firkins does not like my putting stance. I'm too cramped. He likes a bit of a 'hit'. He also says my stroke is overlong. Malins, meanwhile, thinks I freeze at address. I look at the hole, back at the ball, look at the hole, look at ball, hole, ball . . .

'It's a miracle you ever hit the thing,' he says.

He makes me roll the ball with my right hand, to see why my judgement of length is so poor. Instead, I roll it with my left. I'm one of those oddities – I write left-handed, I bat right-handed, I bowl left-handed, I play squash right-handed.

'Perhaps you should putt left-handed,' Malins suggests. I give it a go. I'm just as useless.

Day 117: Whisper it – I'm not one to tempt fate – but I have just had two really good days. I can't remember having felt quite so healthy for years. I've felt . . . well . . . almost normal, to be honest. Not that I remember what normal feels like. But I haven't felt tired and I haven't had to sleep, either in the morning or afternoon. I've even kept up with Emma. Sort of.

I went to one of my NHS meetings the other day and they gave me a book on 'pacing'. It's a simple idea. When I have energy – between 8.00 and 8.30 a.m., usually – I tend to feel so elated that I roar about. I rough and tumble with Emma. I'm the monster, and I chase her about the house. If she's in a really brave mood, we draw the curtains and turn off the lights and she screams in petrified delight. I catch her and she laughs tears, gets her breath back and: 'Again, again!' By 8.31 I'm dead beat.

Pacing means rationing my available energy. Don't get over-excited every time you feel vaguely human. Potter along on an even keel. Sit down and close your eyes now and then. Stop sprinting. Turn your day into a pedestrian jog. It seems to work.

Day 118: I'm giving up pacing. Or rather, Emma's giving it up for me. She explains over breakfast.

'I want you to be the monster again,' she says.

'But then Daddy will have to take morning and afternoon naps,' I explain in my perfectly paced, monotone, monochrome voice.

'I don't mind,' she replies. 'You can sleep when I'm at school. Now chase me.'

Day 122: Are beards always this itchy? Why do people bother? What are they trying to hide?

I'm back at Burhill for the first time AA (After Andrew). Martin's club is grand and imposing. The car park's full of Daimlers, Rolls-Royces, busy butlers and immaculate, clean-shaven chauffeurs. I hide my battered Seat near the trades-man's entrance.

I'm not here to beat Martin. That's not going to happen. It's more about setting a benchmark before The Brothers' Match.

To be honest, everything's playing into my hands. Roger's playing more cricket at the moment, although he's allowed himself to be talked into a golf game next week. Matthew's concentrating on squash. Martin's the dark horse. He's not a natural sportsman but he's cornered all the brains. He's currently playing to 14 or 15 and the trend is downwards.

Martin's brainpower, though, has always confused me when it comes to golf. This is someone who appeared on *University Challenge* while still eating rusks and who's got cleverer ever since. He finishes crosswords before the news-paper's delivered, makes jokes about chemical kinetics, speaks thirteen foreign languages and knows the names of all the Greek and Roman gods. So why hasn't he cracked golf?

Years back, he invited me to take part in a four-ball. The group was completed by a surgeon and a high-flying German business executive. These were men of wealth, stature and substance. They all loved the game and their golf bags bristled with brands. Yet you could not have found a quirkier collection of swings than was displayed on that 1st tee. As our drives flew off in all directions I could not help reflecting that if these brilliant minds weren't adept enough to unlock the game's secret, then what hope the rest of us?

Martin takes to the 1st tee. My elder brother does not turn his shoulders much, he sways laterally and has a flat plane. He looks as flexible as an ironing board. But he still gives the ball a decent crack. Invariably, he sends it between 220 and 240 yards straight up the fairway. He's rarely spectacularly good, but never, ever spectacularly bad. And he's deadly from inside 100 yards.

I outdrive him by 20 yards, hit the green with my second and lose the hole with three putts. By the time I've picked up my ball Martin has already teed off again. He plays at a ferocious lick. I suppose if your mind works quickly, your body gets sucked along in the slipstream. Martin never takes time to smell the roses. He's already run them over with his motorised trolley.

The first hole sets the pattern. Martin doesn't relinquish his lead, even though I play above myself. I'm two behind at the turn and that's where I stay until the 18th.

Martin pars it to finish on 14 over. I hammer my drive into a tree, Old Tom Morris snorts in derision – 'it just had to happen, I just knew he'd lose it just when it matters!' – and I make a quadruple bogey; 20 over – another of those 'if only' rounds. If only I had tried to be a bit less ambitious . . . If only I could handle fast greens and tougher courses. If only . . .

Still, now I know. To beat Martin, I'm going to have to find seven shots.

In the bar, he pays for everything and tells me about his holiday plans. I drink Guinness as quickly as I can.

Day 124: Next up, Roger. Different kettle of fish altogether.

As the youngest brother, Roger rarely appeared on my radar when we were young. Actually, none of them did. Martin was an adult from the age of five – that's months, not years. Whenever we had visitors, the rest of us gambolled around the garden while Martin conversed with the adults. We were never going to bond, not unless I ditched *Andy Pandy* for *The Economist*. Matthew and Roger, meanwhile, were inseparable. I became an only child.

In adulthood, though, Roger and I have grown closer. We've often lived within a stone's throw of each other. Roger's an actor. He's no longer, however, a golfer. He used to beat me regularly. He'd drive his woods and irons with a controlled fade, then chip and putt neatly. He'd get himself out of the mire, whatever the depth of mud. But now his golf swing looks more like an off-drive.

So I fancy my chances. We're playing Paxhill. I sense my first win of the year.

Roger's easy-going enough. Golf, though, brings out the worst in him, as it does in so many, with its promise of perfection so publicly betrayed. He arrives, anticipating a frustrating morning. Understandably but illogically, he would like to perform as well as he used to. He's playing under duress, to please me.

I proceed to play the best round of my life, even if a rash of temporary greens make the course shorter than usual. I score 14 over. Roger is equally delighted with his 18 over.

It's my day from the first hole. I follow a decent drive with a five-iron which pitches in front of the green. It must have rolled on. Only, we can't find it. What an absurd, unfair game. I am about to set off back down the fairway when we unearth the ball in a rabbit hole. I chip on and one-putt for par.

My putting's a revelation. I nail a 30-footer and have five one-putts on the way in. I take thirty putts to my usual thirty-six. Roger's impressed. Eureka! Putting's the secret of golf! I text Gilroy and he, too, is impressed. Or perhaps I misread impression for incredulity.

TEN

TALKING TO A US OPEN CHAMPION

'My favourite shots are the practice swing and the
concededputt. The rest can never be mastered'

— *Lord Robertson*

Weight: 13st 5lb
Waist measurement: 37in
Diet: Better than Craig Stadler's.
Alcohol: Still better than John Daly's.
Chronic Fatigue: Back to one hour's sleep a day.
Beard: Straggly.
Official handicap: 24
Rounds: 8
Average score per round: 21.75 over
Longest drive: 245 yards (21 December, Goodwood, 18th)
Range balls: 2,160
Self-belief: 7/10
And the secret of golf is . . . putting.

1 February: Day 125, 240 to go.

8 a.m. Emma can make me laugh one minute and break my
heart the next. She doesn't know she's doing it. When she finds
out, I'll be putty in her small, pink, perfectly formed hands. I
must keep this a secret. For at least fifteen more years.

This morning we discuss her geography project. She lists
the biggest countries in the world: 'Russia, Canada, China,
United America States, Australia and . . . and . . . Walnut.' I nod

— once my slow-witted brain has made the link between Walnut and Brazil — while heroically keeping a straight face.

Half an hour later she inexplicably gets the wobbles at the school gates, and she turns to me and begins to cry. She wants to stay with me and she clings to my leg. I know I have to be strong, so I prise open her fingers as tenderly as I can and hand her over to her teacher. Emma looks back accusingly at me over her shoulder through hot, anguished tears as she's led away. I turn on my heel and mutter: 'Don't look back, don't look back . . . ' And I don't. I walk away, a knife through the heart.

It stays there all day, until pick-up. Emma skips out of school, laughing delightfully. She has no idea what she puts me through. I don't suppose she ever will.

9 a.m. I stare at a photo sequence of Nick Faldo's golf swing. I try to say: 'I want to be Faldo.' Only, the words don't come out.

I want desperately to revere all things Faldo but it's hard. I've never warmed to the man. How can you be drawn to someone whose golf — and personality, I sometimes feel — was formulaically concocted in a laboratory?

I've always been a Seve Ballesteros devotee. There was never anything remotely test-tube about Ballesteros. If there's such a thing as a natural golfer — and I still find golf about as natural as Russia without the vodka — then this raging, coruscating, elemental Spaniard's your man.

Like all geniuses, he defies comprehension. One minute he's in the Royal Lytham car park, his ball bouncing amid the hubcaps, and the next he's holing a 30-foot birdie putt on the way to the 1979 Open. At times he played like a 24-handicapper yet still somehow squeezed the ball into the hole. It must have been through sheer force of personality.

Deep down, I'm sure all hackers prefer the Latin Ballesteros to the Nordic Faldo. We empathise with the erratic. We prefer our champions flawed. We prefer Mickelson to Woods, Daly to Furyk, Palmer to Nicklaus. We lean towards heroes who reflect something of us. And, of course, we all think of ourselves as misunderstood artists.

But I can't rid myself of the suspicion that that is exactly why we remain hackers. Flashes of brilliance may work for geniuses but I'm not sure it works for mortals. We just end up losing a lot of balls.

I didn't think I'd ever admit it but I fear Faldo's the way forward. Faldo's cold-fish functional. Faldo hit the ball monotonously, meticulously, slide-rule straight. Faldo exemplified the value of mundane repetition over divine inspiration. He built a swing to survive an ice age. Ballesteros blew up and burnt out like a meteor, mislaying his genius somewhere along the way.

I go back to the Faldo pictures and try again to betray Ballesteros.

In truth, though, I'm already halfway to thirty pieces of silver. Gilroy's putting has seen to that. I've seen the light. Good golf is precision. It's repetition. It's roundhead, not cavalier. It's successful tedium.

So what do I find boring, apart from putting? Chipping and pitching, of course. I must learn to chip and pitch.

Day 127: I've been getting strange looks from the VSPMs over the past few days. I'm unsure why. I'm wearing the same jeans and the same coat. Admittedly, they've seen better days, but then so have I.

Mia, paratrooper sister of one of Emma's classmates,

provides the answer. She runs up and points at the unkempt growth on my face.

'Ha ha, Tony's a tramp!'

I examine my would-be beard in the car mirror. I think it looks rather distinguished, naval even. Apart from the bald patches.

I go shopping – I need flour and butter for tonight's macaroni cheese. When I get home, I realise that it wasn't on my 'Things To Do' list. So I add 'Shopping' to the list, then cross it out again. Pathetic, really, but it makes me feel good.

The macaroni cheese, incidentally, looks like porridge and tastes like wallpaper paste. I think it's quirkily challenging but Jan phones up Domino's. They know her by name now.

Day 128: I return to the garage, delve through the cobwebs and emerge clutching Dave Pelz.

Pelz would get on perfectly with Faldo. Pelz used to work with NASA. He's a scientist. I can't believe he has an artistic bone in his body. But you can't deny the quality of his graphs and spreadsheets.

Pelz spent years lurking on the sidelines of the PGA Tour, watching players and scribbling down numbers in a notebook. By the end, he reckoned he'd discovered something. A few pros listened. And so Pelz became a guru.

I bought his *Short Game Bible* a few years ago. I was captivated. I even considered devoting myself to his system. But then I'd been distracted by a gadget promising 340-yard drives within a month or your money back (I didn't get either – the 340 yards or my £19.99).

Pelz argues – I compress hundreds of data-laden pages into a pistachio shell – that the average golfer has a bunch of clubs designed to hit between 120 and 200 yards but that, because he rarely hits straight, he misses the green anyway. In contrast, he has only two clubs, a pitching-wedge and a sand-wedge, to deal with the scoring zone – 120 yards and in.

Pelz advocates throwing away a few wayward long irons in favour of two extra wedges. Learn three formulaic, different-length shots with each wedge and, hey presto, you'll have twelve shots within 120 yards to attack the pin.

The alternative is to 'sense' or 'feel' your wedge distances. It's never worked for me. I have the feel of a be-mittened polar explorer with frostbite. I like the idea of a pre-programmed shot, and a pre-ordained distance. My only gripe is the number of pages it takes Pelz to make his point. But bibles, by their nature, tend to be heavy on the preaching.

Day 129: I get an email. Would I like another game with my ex-Reuters colleagues later this month? Yes, I would.

Day 131: I go to Paxhill range for two hours. I'm the only person there.

I now have four eBay wedges, from 48 to 60 degrees. Perfect. I hit ten balls with the lob wedge, using a 7.30 back-swing. I pace out the distance and then repeat the process with a 9 o'clock backswing, followed by a 10.30. I repeat the process with each club.

I have doubts, though. There's a wind, for a start. What effect will that have? And it's muddy, so there's no roll. And my pitching-wedge and 52-degree wedge seem to go the same distance.

Day 132: I return to the range. I'm the only person there. I repeat the process. All my distances have changed overnight. Everything goes further. Hell's teeth. Just keep at it.

I spend more time practising my pitching in two days than in the previous seven years.

At school, we run into sister-in-law Hilary and her brood. She asks about the golf. It's tough, I say. I don't really understand the game yet. I certainly don't understand golfers.

'I mean, can you think of any other hobby where people persevere despite being patently hopeless? I know it's just an excuse for a pint and a chat for some, but why not just have the pint and chat? Why bother with the golf?'

Hilary likes dancing.

'Golf sounds as technical as tap,' she says. 'If you can't get tap dancing right, then you wouldn't bother continuing. There'd be no point. It would sound and look awful.'

My point exactly. I want a nice-looking golf swing. In this I'm an absolutist. What's the point of resembling a drunk trying to swat mosquitoes with a newspaper in a phone box? Golf courses deserve a little beauty in return. I make a mental note. Never take up tap dancing.

Day 133: Malins, I learn, is not a Pelzian.

'It's too mechanical,' he says. 'You should trust your instincts.'

He gets me to pitch at different flags while relying on feel. I do surprisingly well. Next he tells me to aim at the 75-yard flag using the Pelz method. That should be a 9 o'clock swing with my 52-degree wedge. I get close. Then Malins shows me the video. I actually swung to 10 o'clock. Give or take a few minutes.

'That's because your instincts sensed that the ball would fall short, so your body compensated,' argues Alastair. 'You thought you were using Pelz's method but actually your feel took over.'

Damnation.

He asks me to throw a ball into his right hand. After a couple of accurate throws, he asks me to concentrate hard on the exact angle of my throwing arm, and the way my elbow and wrist move. The next throw flies high and way off target. Alastair's point? I was more accurate when instinctive. Over-analysis stinks.

I go away confused. Bloody golf teachers. Wish they'd make up their minds.

Day 134: I read on the Internet that Pelz is Mickelson's short-game coach. Mickelson, the world's greatest 'touch' player, is using a mechanical method? Does that make sense? In the end, you pays your money and takes your choice.

Day 135: My beard has stopped itching but I'm beginning to suck on the moustache. How are you meant to trim these things? The kitchen scissors are too big. Nail clippers?

James and I squeeze in eighteen holes before Emma's swimming class. She's having trouble mastering the breast-stroke. For some reason, she prefers swimming along the bottom of the pool rather than on the surface.

I score 14 over, for the second time in a row. Brilliant! I've dropped to a new plateau! Except that it doesn't feel too different. I seem to cut and top as much as ever. I just score better. Odd.

James plays to 11. He thinks my wrists still roll. My divots still point left. Six out of nine chips, though, get to within 8 feet and, for the very first time, I get up and down from a bunker.

Back home, I muse.

Clearly, chipping, pitching and putting are the secret to golf. You can get around with a pretty flaky long game but salvage a score with some neat approaches and a clutch of one-putts. It's that simple. Apparently, around 65 per cent of our shots consist of pitches, chips and putts. (Pelz has worked out, incidentally, that the 42-yard shot is the hardest of all. To which I say: 'Get a life'.)

There's a problem, though. Where do people practise this secret? I'm privileged. I have Paxhill range all to myself. But whereto Man In The Street? Public ranges are no good. The only guides are the 50 and 100 boards. Are they accurate? Are they yards or metres? And what are range balls made of? Something similar to my coagulated macaroni cheese.

What people need is real golf balls and a 120-yard field of their own. And if that isn't possible, then they need a cheap, well-maintained, near-deserted par-three course.

One on the Internet catches my eye. If I can't spend my year travelling to Florida or St Andrews, I should at least try to spend one Emma-free day outside Sussex. The par-three course I choose is in Birmingham. Former US Open champion Alison Nicholas runs the place.

Day 137: Weekend at Granpy and Nanny's in the wilds of Somerset. The house is full of fishing gear, tawny owl feathers, dog leads, mud-encrusted boots, air rifles and bags of compost and animal feed.

Jan's happy because she loves visiting her parents and the countryside of her youth. Emma loves it because Granpy and Nanny show her the chickens, the ferrets and frog spawn, they show her carrots and cauliflowers, oak and sycamore leaves, they talk about otters a lot – an awful lot – and take her on long walks with Baloo, the softest dog that ever lived.

I love it because Granpy and Nanny go on long walks with Emma and Jan and Baloo, leaving me to stay indoors with large packets of chocolate biscuits. Bizarrely, I also enjoy my chats with brother-in-law John. Every now and again he says something surprisingly astute.

John's a countryman. He carves walking-stick handles out of sheep horn. He can identify a bird of prey 1,000 feet up. He can smell rain and sense a storm. Mainly, though, he's a fisherman. A scratch handicap fisherman. He has photographs of pike in his wallet, trout magazines under his bed and posters of sea bass rather than naked women motorbike mechanics on his bedroom wall (why is it that women mechanics wear so little?). He goes fishing to Ireland and Canada to meet people just like him (a frightening prospect, although it's probably best to keep them all together in one place). He can talk fish way beyond pub closing time. Remarkably, he's as boring on his subject as I am on mine.

We make a peculiar partnership. The unwritten rule is that I allow him five minutes to expound on the best way to tie a Black Highrider sedge fly so long as he gives me the next five to ponder on buried lies in greenside bunkers. We take turns to talk past each other. Occasionally, we meet in the middle.

He tells of fishermen with 'all the gear, no idea' and I talk of players full of laughable theories but devoid of common sense. He responds with fishermen with empty keep nets who offer unsolicited advice to neighbours busily reeling in shoals faster than a North Sea trawler. I switch to wrist cock and lag and he counters with loading up the tip of the rod.

As a form of communication, it sort of works.

One thing, though, he does not get.

'You see, Tony, I have a great time and I end up with a bagful of fish,' he says. 'You have a great time and end up with . . . well, nothing.'

I have a ready riposte.

'Remember when you taught me how to fly fish? I really enjoyed the sensation, the movement, the art. I loved the way the line flew out across the lake. It's the same with golf. I just want to hit pure shots.'

John considers this. 'Look, there's no point fishing without fish. I like casting too, and making my own flies. But the point's the fish. So golf must be about scoring, not hitting nicely. And even then, to be honest, I don't really see the point. Not without fish.'

And with that he returns to carving, skinning a rabbit, polishing binoculars or teasing sea salt and algae from his eyebrows.

Day 140: Alison Nicholas is about as tall as a thimble. I'd expected more for my money. She wouldn't look out of place on a mantelpiece, or dangling from a key ring.

She's also on the quiet side of self-effacing. I get the impression she's still finding her feet as a golf teacher, however odd that may sound. She won eighteen professional tournaments, including the 1997 US Open, during a twenty-year career ending in 2004. She appeared in a bagful of Solheim Cups. She has everything to shout about, but chooses not to.

The other thing that strikes me is her eyes. She manages to look shy, knowing and amused at the same time.

It's surprisingly easy to book a golf lesson with a former US Open champion. You just phone up. We meet at her golf academy at Queslett Park golf range, just outside Birmingham. I arrive early to play the par-three course. There are only a few other people out, while a barrage of noise rings out from the fifty-eight-bay, two-tier range. I pitch, chip and putt my way round, then go around again, until I've lost my four balls.

I tell Nicholas I'd like to work on my pitching. She asks me to hit some shots. She's pleasantly surprised.

'But you're pulling a bit. Try to follow through on a straighter line. That will also give your shots more height, and they'll get more spin. You're rolling over the ball a fraction. Weaken your grip, and think of your left shoulder going up rather than round.'

As a bonus, she teaches me a chip shot. She cuts across the ball with a soft left arm and it fizzes to a stop on the second bounce. She has the ball on a string.

We retire for a hot drink.

I like the course, I tell Nicholas. Par-three courses are in short supply. It's the part of golf that nobody practises.

'That's right, they don't,' she says. 'But to a tour pro 100 yards and in is massive. It's where you save your shots. You don't hit eighteen greens in regulation every day, whoever you are. I'm not sure I ever did – well, once perhaps. Let's say your average pro hits fourteen greens in regulation. That means they have to get up and down four times.'

Will I be able to lose five more shots in the next seven months and score in single figures, I ask?

'Yes. But you're going to have to work on your short game.'

Hard work is a Nicholas mantra.

'Based on my teaching experience, you can improve people up to a point but if you want dramatic improvements you're going to have to stick to doing one particular move right, for however long that takes, before moving on,' she says, sounding worryingly like Pharro.

'But people want golf served up to them in half an hour. That puts incredible pressure on the teacher. A lot of students won't be told. They think they know more about the swing than I do. They've read all the books and watched the videos. I spend lots of time just trying to get rid of all the stuff in their heads.

'I found it frustrating at first but my patience has improved. I try to get people to understand what they're taking on. I ask: "Do you think this is going to take a short time?" I encourage questions. It can be great fun, when people are positive about taking on the challenge of developing a new action.

'Learning's hard but you have to stick with it. I did. I wanted to win a major so my coach went about changing my swing. We overhauled my grip, which was too weak, and we changed my takeaway to stop me picking the club up. I hit some horrendous shots at first, but my goal was to win that major. And I did. But it took me two years to get where I wanted. There were lots of tears.'

Nicholas took up the game at seventeen. She'd always been sporty. Her success, though, depended in part on her father's foresight. He let her leave school and funded her for four years. After that, it would be up to her. First, though, he stipulated six months of lessons.

'I wasn't allowed on the course but I could practise as much as I wanted. Most people just want to play but they haven't learnt the basics, let alone what to do at impact. I did half swings for what seemed like an eternity. But when I got out on the course things happened quickly. My handicap came down from 30 to 11 in the first year. Within four years, I'd got to scratch.'

The rest is history. Today Nicholas concentrates on running her academy and on teaching, media and charity work and speaking engagements.

It's getting late and there's a long drive back. I fire out my million-dollar questions: Is there one correct method to teach golf? Why are average handicaps not falling? And what about a secret?

Nicholas smiles.

'There are lots of different methods but I'm not sure too much is revolutionary. I'm not saying nothing's new but there's lots of repackaging. Teachers today say golf is all about big muscles. Well, that was being said in the 1930s and 40s. I have all my grandfather's books and it's in there. But you can't ignore the arms or the hands. Your hands are the only contact with the club.'

As for handicaps, well: 'Yes, I've seen those statistics as well. Will average handicaps get better? I don't know. It's a good question. As you've found out, people may think it's all about natural talent but we all have to work at it. It's a difficult game, no question. There are so many facets.

'I don't believe there's one single secret but I'm more and more convinced that the physical aspect is fundamental. If you can't hold your posture, then it doesn't make any difference how much you understand or get taught. Some people have appalling posture. They just can't get into the right positions. You have to have core stability.

'You let older players use their arms and hands a bit more, of course, rather than rotating the trunk. But it's surprising how inflexible people are. I suppose it's down to sedentary lifestyles. Too much Nintendo.'

She says I'm doing well. 'Just try not to be so tense. Tension, whether mental or physical, will affect your game. About 80 per cent of players are too tense. You're thinking too hard.'

I ask for one last piece of gold-dust advice.

'The short game,' she replies. 'Chipping, putting, bunker play, pitching and distance control. That's it.'

I drive home, feeling great, if a little sedentary. I don't even have a Nintendo as an excuse. So the secret of golf – apart from rolling wrists, of course, and the short game and hard work – is my physique? I'm not sure this is good news.

Day 141: As the start of a concerted fitness drive, I eat vegetables for lunch and dinner, four bananas, drink three glasses of water and I do twelve sit-ups and seventeen-and-a-half press-ups.

Day 144: Back in the garage. This time I reappear with Vivien Saunders.

I'd never heard of her until my brother Matthew lent me one of her short-game videos a few years back. I found it ridiculous.

I had several objections. For a start, the video seemed to date back to the early 1800s. Did people really wear jumpers like that back then? Second, she looked like Delia Smith – primly proper and with impossibly small feet.

Worst of all, Saunders said that chipping was just like putting. She made it sound so simple and unfeasibly straight-forward. Which was clearly absurd.

A conversation with Matthew, however, prompts a rethink.

'Yes, funny little video, isn't it?' he says, after I promise to return it, four years late. 'But she knows what she's on about, whoever she is. When I got down to single figures I was using her technique.'

So I watch the video again. It still seems absurdly dated and plum-in-your-mouth. For no obvious reason, I give it a go.

Day 147: Paxhill range. I am the only person there. I pitch. All my distances change again. At least my chipping's improving. I'm getting quite canny with my seven-iron from the fringe. Saunders would be proud. If she were still alive, which she probably isn't. Nobody I speak to has heard of her. Until Firkins.

'Oh yes,' he says, 'she was quite a player in her time.'

Oh, so she was a player?

Firkins, though, is more intent on scrutinising my new chipping style. He doesn't like the idea of me taking advice from someone else, but he says yes, it's fine, the putt-chip works in certain situations.

Day 149: February stops raining for a few hours.

Bad lesson with Alastair. My takeaway, he says, is still not right. I feel like punching him but instead reply a shade haughtily that, all things considered, I may have to accept that I'm incapable of getting it 100 per cent correct. I'll live with 99.8.

It's not that simple, he says. 'This is fundamental.' I have to master it. I've improved, but wrist roll will always affect my accuracy and distance. I sulk, then text James for a game.

I go round in my third 14 over par in a row and feel happier. Things can't be that bad, whatever Alastair says. I hit straight enough and I putt and chip nicely. In fact, it could easily have been better. One drive gets stuck under the lip of a fairway bunker and one short putt lips out on a temporary green.

There's another bonus. James takes an interest in my new pitching method and an even greater interest in my clubs after I explain that my 48- and 52-degree wedges fly the same distance. He scurries off, returning ten minutes later.

'Your 52's fine,' he announces. 'But your pitching-wedge is actually 51 degrees. There's your problem. Effectively, you're carrying two identical clubs. I've adjusted it back to 48. That should sort it. No charge. A pint? Why, thank you very much.'

Day 152: I'm sitting at Poult Wood, beer in hand and glistening with pride. I'm very keen to dissect my latest round in minute detail. Mitch and Dave, though, seem less enthusiastic, while Pat has excused herself and set off for home.

Typical. I've just enjoyed the most remarkable round of my life and nobody cares a jot. Mitch wants to talk about his triathlon training. Dave shows off the plans for his new conservatory.

I want to talk about my 12 over. Pat, a beginner, and I have just trounced Dave and Mitch in our Stableford head-to-head. I drove more consistently than ever before. No lost balls, no out of bounds. There's also sweet revenge at the par-four 16th. Mitch, as usual, calls me a blouse and then loses his first two drives into the trees. I go for a five-iron, a nine-iron and a par. I walk off wearing my most superior smile.

Totting up my score, I find four more shots I could have saved, on a perfect day. Suddenly, for the first time, single figures seems possible. However hard I try, though, I can't elicit a word of praise from Mitch.

'Are you sure you scored 12 over?' he says. 'I mean, it's not as if you hit any remarkable shots.'

Initially, I'm miffed. Then, gradually, I'm intrigued. He's right. I didn't do anything astounding. I was merely consistently OK. Mitch felt that, on a good day, he could have matched any of my shots. There were no 300-yard drives, no five-irons to 2 feet, no magical rescues from fairway bunkers, chip-ins nor 40-foot putts. All I did was to avoid howlers.

There you have it. The secret of golf — well, 12-handicap golf, anyway — is avoiding disaster. The key is not what you do but what you don't. The key's your bad shots, not your good. You don't need to be brilliant, Mitch. Just stay out of the trees.

ELEVEN
MR BLOBBY'S BACK IN BIRMINGHAM

'Golf is an awkward set of bodily contortions designed
to produce a graceful result'

— *Tommy Armour*

Weight: 13st 3lb
Waist measurement: 36½in
Diet: All I lack is willpower.
Alcohol: Red wine is good for you – *The Wine News* magazine.
Chronic Fatigue: Steady.
Beard: Distinguished (from where I'm looking).
Official handicap: 24
Rounds: 11
Average score per round: 19.45 over
Average score over last ten rounds: 20.2 over
Average score over last five: 14.2 over
Eagles: 0
Longest drive: 245 yards (21 December, Goodwood, 18th)
Number of range balls hit: 2,500
Self-belief: 7/10
And the secret of golf is . . . fine-tune your short game, sell
     the Nintendo, avoid disasters.

1 March, Day 153: 212 to go.
I'm not fat. I'm just fatter, that's all. Or rounder, rather. Yes, I
prefer that. I'm a shade rounder than I'd like. But I'm certainly
not fat. Not much, anyway.

Jan says she knows why. My relationship with food has

changed since I became a house husband. I now treat food as a comfort rather than a necessity. Jan says I eat to fill my day, not my stomach.

The woman's talking nonsense. If I do snack a shade more than I once did — and yes, let's face it, I may do — then it's because I've uncovered a secret known only to homebound parents.

Chocolate biscuits can talk.

It doesn't matter where Jan conceals them, they still communicate with me. 'We're here, behind the bread bin, over here, over here . . . '

The chocolate biscuits in Roy's house also talk, apparently. Roy's between jobs. For now, he's a house husband too. On Sunday mornings we stretch out like beached whales in the kids' pool at the sports centre. Our daughters thrash about at the far end, near the pink elephant slide. We throw them cursory glances. They don't appear to be drowning. Roy and I remain semi-submerged, noses and stomachs breaking the surface. We enjoy a few precious moments of being almost out of sight, almost out of mind. We talk biscuits.

Actually, we talk lots of things. We discuss the possibility of perhaps one day getting fit — that's seriously fit, not just occasional-jog-down-to-the-pub fit. We talk house husbandry — is a house husband a failed man impersonating a dutiful woman or some superior modern mutation? Roy leans to the former, I to the latter. We talk about the guilt of not earning a regular wage. We wonder whether work defines us. I don't miss my erstwhile colleagues that much, I say, but there's something to be said for the daily banter, however banal. Roy, meanwhile, pines for a desk, a manager's authority and four office walls.

'You just haven't got used to the isolation yet,' I tell him. 'It

takes time. Talking of fitness, I've just contacted a physiotherapist offering a golf programme. I'm off to see him in a
couple of weeks.'

'Why not just go to the gym? You're a member, aren't you?'

No, I'm lapsed. Jan and I signed up for a month's promotion.
Jan went once and got waylaid by the coffee bar, while I managed
three visits. Jan didn't provide a reason for giving up. The
quality of the coffee, presumably. As for me, I thought I'd get a
six-pack just by signing up. Unreasonably, I was expected to lift
weights, and run about, and sweat and things. I also found the
swing doors rather difficult to push open.

Roy and I bask until our finger ends wrinkle.

'Fancy a cup of tea — and biscuits — after school drop-off
tomorrow?' says Roy. 'Oh, and by the way, your beard's
rubbish.'

Roy needs to get back to work. He's falling off the face of his
own self-esteem. I need to get to the golf range.

Day 161: Knightsbridge. Déjà vu. Still rolling my wrists and
still no Hugh Grant. It's hard for us to synchronise our busy
diaries. I ask Wilkinson to suggest an April meeting. He'll try.
I've given up asking Wilkinson for an interview. It would be
easier to staple blancmange to the ceiling.

Home. I plan. I won't go back to Pharro this month. March
will be about playing. I'm undergoing something of a U-turn.
The search for the perfect golf swing is all very well but I
simply have to learn how to score. I have to learn how to limit
the damage. I have to plot my way around Paxhill. Where do I
normally leak shots? And what about mapping the breaks on
each green?

I start scribbling. Soon there are Post-It Notes all over the house – lists of swing thoughts (twelve to date), golf secrets (about twenty-five) and diagrams of fairways, bunkers and water hazards. They get mixed up with my 'Things to do' lists.

I retrieve my Paxhill and Poult Wood scorecards. There are eleven, spanning five months. I've hit 32, 25 and 27 over to get my official opening handicap, followed by 22, 19, 18, 17, 14, 14, 14, 12. That's an average of 19.45. Over the past five rounds, I'm down to 14.2. Blimey. That's a solid downward trend. I've lost ten shots – in eleven rounds!

How, exactly? Four I ascribe to course management. I've stopped trying to hit my driver out of fairway bunkers, bend Garcia-style shots out of tree roots and blast four-irons 200 yards out of thigh-high rough. And I've stopped believing that I habitually hit seven-irons 165 yards just because it happened once (I think the ball must have hit a drain cover).

Then there's the steadier wrists, the improved putting and pitching and chipping. All I need do now is get fit, learn a few mental tricks and drive better and I'll be in single figures. I'll collect a raft of personal statistics. I'll record the number of fairways I hit, the greens reached in regulation, the percentage of chips to within 8 feet and my putts per round. I'll categorise my shots as brilliant, very good, good, OK, bad, very bad and rubbish. I'll draw graphs and make spreadsheets. Doddle.

Day 169: Not a doddle. Not a doddle at all. Disastrously, incomprehensibly non-doddle. I've played three rounds in the last week and nothing makes sense. I score 19, 13 and 21 over. So much for science. My belief in mechanical, structured, programmed, inevitable improvement explodes spectacularly.

The worst thing about the first round is that I have no idea why it happens. I know I slice everything, even my practice swings. But what causes it? Can I blame the cross-wind? Do I grip too tightly? One minute I seem fine and sixty seconds later I can't hit barn doors with banjos.

From the 8th to the 12th I go triple bogey, bogey, triple, double, triple. Twelve over in five holes, a run including three out of bounds! Golf then mocks me. I've all but given up when my slice, suddenly and for no apparent reason, departs the scene of the crime.

For the record, I hit six of fourteen fairways, five greens in regulation, chip to within 8 feet on five of eleven occasions and take thirty-four putts. What does that tell me? I can't hit straight.

Perhaps I'm wrong but I sense James is taking secret delight in my tribulations. Perhaps he's been waiting for golf to bite back. Perhaps he thinks I've been having things my own way for too long. Perhaps he knows golf's more difficult than I realise. Perhaps he's right.

The equally inexplicable 13 over, two days later, is with Roger. I start nicely, then make a ridiculous mess of the straightforward par-five 3rd. I hit a nice drive, concentrating on 80 per cent power – as recommended by Freddie Couples (Golf Channel) – while chanting 'peace, harmony, relax, relax' – as read in one of my golf books. A five-iron leaves an 80-yard pitch. Birdie chance. I blade the ball over the green into the river.

But I hang on. I'm fading my woods. I live with it. I play within myself. Roger, meanwhile, fails to reproduce the miracle of his previous round. This time he plays to type. On the 10th green he announces he would rather be at home, reading the newspaper. He turns dark and murderous. His much-anticipated day off turns into a grind. Only golf can do this. They say it reflects your true self. Either that or it's just plain vicious.

I, meanwhile, am borderline elated. I hit seven fairways, seven greens in regulation and chip six out of nine to within 8 feet. Thirty-five putts. I know there's more to come. Four more shots, I tell Jan, and the beard goes. Any day now.

My third round – more inexplicable still – is with my old friend Mike. Mike expects nothing from golf. You only have to look at his physique and his swing to see why. Mike is short, cerebral, analytical and logical. Except when it comes to golf. Content with the vagaries of the game, he hacks happily, enjoying the walk, while discussing computer programming, music and eighteenth-century German philosophers.

Mike and I met at university. We also shared our year out in Germany. Mike was rushed home almost as soon as he'd arrived after a chest x-ray revealed a shadow. Cancer was muted but it was a false alarm. Mike had had a collapsed lung since birth. He saw no need to cut back on his smoking. Later, we bought some aerosol cans – we chose red paint and the shopkeeper asked us whether it was for our Mercedes or BMW – and sprayed 'One lung is better than none' on the Berlin Wall, next to 'Geoff Boycott is God', a few hundred yards away from Checkpoint Charlie.

I'm keen to show Mike how I'm improving. So keen that I play horribly. Oddly, though, amidst the dross are some real gems – a 175-yard four-iron tee shot to 4 inches and a 100-yard wedge approach to a foot. I blast a wind-assisted 272-yard drive on the 18th which beggars belief. But the rest is too horrible to contemplate. My bad shots land behind trees, in pot holes and ditches, plug in the face of bunkers or are caught in mid-air and carried off by golden eagles. The beard stays.

An uneasy feeling is taking hold. Perhaps golf really is unfair. You hear it chuntered regularly, albeit by moon-worshiping high handicappers, the sort who say: 'I'd like to play my normal game just once.' I've always regarded it as an excuse – blame the game and absolve yourself. But what if it were true? What if there really was some malevolent golfing deity? It happened to Ballesteros. And what about Ian Baker-Finch? He won the 1991 Open but soon after, ensnared in swing changes, he saw his career implode. For no obvious reason, he no longer seemed able to play. Then his confidence melted. He'd return in hope rather than expectation to the 1997 Open only to shoot 92. 'I felt like I was walking naked,' he said.

No. I banish the idea. Golf is a science. If I'm scientific, I'll crack the code.

James joins us for a drink.

'You're thinking too hard and you're trying too hard, Tony,' he says. 'Relax.'

Day 171: The great thing about Steven Harris is not who he is, but who he is not. Steven Harris is not Arnold Schwarzenegger. Nor am I, of course – I'm Mr Blobby – but I still feel relieved.

Harris does not have a washboard for a midriff. In fact, when I meet him, he looks as if he's eaten as many pies as I have. He's not fat – in fact he's stocky and powerful – but he's far from chiselled. He looks comfortable. Normal. He's also immediately friendly, accessible and unassuming. I feel I've known him for ages.

I arrive at his BodyGolf physiotherapy clinic, on the edge of Birmingham, without preconceptions or preconditions. I know I'm unfit and overweight. Martin recently bought me a

Lycra sports skin to wear under my golf shirts. It feels fantastic but reveals more than I'd wish. Jan laughs out loud. I wear it behind closed doors, after the 9 o'clock watershed.

I know, of course, what's required. If I ever write a diet book, I'll entitle it: *Stop Eating All the Biscuits, You Fat Bastard*. But golf's another matter. What's golf fitness? Look at the Seniors Tour. Happily paunched, they still play sublimely.

I skim-read some less-than-enthralling readers' letters in *Physiotherapist's Monthly* in the waiting room while thinking of my brother-in-law. Every New Year, John resolves to get fit. His version of fitness is the six-pack. Religiously, he does press-ups and crunches and then, one blazing June evening, he has a beer with his mates. Then he has another, and another and he goes home, walks straight past his weights and doesn't touch them until the following January. John, as I recall, has never even had a one-pack.

And I think of Mitch, pounding along country lanes, scaling mountains and thrashing up and down swimming pools. His version of fitness is stamina. He gets bored practising golf but he never tires of running around in large, pointless circles.

I no longer have a version of fitness.

It was Alison Nicholas's comments about golfers' physical incapacities which spurred me to find Harris on the Internet. So Mr Blobby is back in Birmingham.

Harris beckons me through.

His most illustrious client is professional golfer and former Ryder Cup player Paul Broadhurst. He'd slipped to 330th in the world rankings and not won for eight years when he came to see Harris in 2004. Two years later he was back in the top fifty with two more victories to his name.

'He had a bad elbow. I was developing an exercise programme

for golfers and asked him to act as my guinea pig,' explains Harris. 'His elbow took three months to sort out, so we had plenty of time together. First I carried out an assessment of his general flexibility and strength. To his surprise, we found he was really restricted or weak in certain areas.

'I gave him exercises for his arms, elbow, forearms and wrist. We also worked on his right hip. It gave way occasionally on his backswing and he'd hit bad shots. We strengthened it and it stopped happening. Sorting that may have saved him one or two shots a round.

'He worked really hard. As a golfer of thirty years' experience, he also helped improve some of the exercises. In his second tournament back, he led the British Masters into the final day. He hadn't led for years. Paul was very, very chuffed. And I was chuffed to bits for him.'

I want to talk on, if only to delay the inevitable. I know I'm going to have to strip off and try to reach my toes (we've lost touch over the years). I know I'm going to be humiliated and I know it's going to hurt.

Harris used to play golf, to a 10 handicap. At first, his only goal was simply to out-hit his mates.

'I took me three years to realise that I'd got things the wrong way round and that direction was the thing. That's when I improved. It's a lesson some men never learn. Perhaps that's why handicaps never come down.'

It was then that his thoughts turned to golf fitness. What could a physiotherapist do for golfers?

'I knew how to test joint and muscle flexibility, so I put together a method of assessment and a set of exercises. At first I was just doing it for myself. It certainly helped. I began to hit the ball down the middle, hit it on the green, then two-putt.

And with that, I got bored. That always happens. Once I master something, I move on. I played for Warwickshire 2nd XI at cricket, then gave up. I learnt the guitar, then gave up. Imagine playing golf all the time – it would drive you mad.'

Enough talk. He tells me to relax.

But I can't. For one thing, I'm desperate not to break wind as Harris bullies my body through circus-act contortions. I shouldn't have eaten those three pasties on the drive up. And I'm also wondering whether this physical stuff is really so necessary to hitting a half decent five-iron?

Apparently, it is. Harris refers back Broadhurst.

'Flexibility gives people the chance to reach their potential. Paul's ability is the key to his success, of course. But if you haven't got the capability to do things, skill isn't enough. It may not be the secret of golf, but it's part of it.'

He slings me on to my back, bends my knee upwards and crushes it into my chest cavity. Mercifully, I do not break wind. I just go puce.

The battering lasts an hour, and includes the inevitable low point.

'Touch your toes,' orders Harris.

I lunge forward determinedly. I fall 6 inches short.

I change back into my civvies feeling like a C-stream schoolboy awaiting his end-of-term Latin report.

'You're rather weak around your abdominals,' Harris concludes. 'It's like the rollocks of a rowing boat. It's the pivot point. If it's strong, your oar movement will be strong. If it's loose, it won't. It's central to the whole movement. That's the analogy I give for core strength.

'Your back muscles are really weak too. And there's your lack of flexibility. You need to be flexible to complete your backswing. It's such a difficult, unnatural position. There are a lot of joint rotations, while you have to keep looking down at the ball. Flexibility isn't really a male thing. Women are much more into elegant movement, bending, yoga, that sort of stuff. Men do strengthening. But too much muscle can cause golfers problems.

'Biceps don't play a big part in the swing but if you build them up they'll try to get a slice of the action. A lot of players use the wrong muscles. Golf's more about triceps, at the back, which straightens your arm. You've got good biceps. They're no use whatsoever. You need stronger forearms.

'Oh, and you also have flat feet. And abnormally short arms.'

All is not doom and gloom, though. Harris offers me a workout DVD, an exercise band and a sliver of hope.

'If you work on this regularly, it should take a few strokes off your handicap.'

I drive home, worrying about my muscle-less stomach, weak back, odd feet, superfluous biceps and abnormal arms. At least I can still reach the steering wheel.

Evening, Internetting. Apparently, I have some 650 muscles in my body, making up half my body weight. And I have more than 230 moveable and semi-moveable joints that could affect my swing. That includes twenty-seven bones in my hand. Humans and giraffes also have the same number of bones in their neck. Which is intriguing but not particularly relevant.

Day 173: I'm tired and I don't give golf a thought. Not a single one. Unheard of. I spend the day sleeping, daydreaming to Radio 4 and wondering why Jan puts up with me.

I was recovering from my first bout of ME twenty-five years ago when I met her while working on a local newspaper. She expressed her affection by throwing paper clips at me (she was the Education Correspondent, while I had the Transport brief). She was in a serious relationship, I in a frivolous one. She wore terrible colours and the most beautiful smile you'll ever see. She had – and still has – brown eyes to die for. When she split from her partner she decamped to Plymouth. In the one romantic gesture of my life, I followed.

Sometimes I wonder if she'd have done better throwing paper clips at the Chief Reporter.

Day 176: I watch Harris's DVD and spend twenty minutes on the living room carpet, grunting. The abdominal crunches are made harder by Emma sitting on my stomach while watching Harry Potter. I try to touch my toes and meet my knees instead. I do a lighter session after Emma's bed-time, while watching The Golf Channel. I determine to do three sessions a week

Day 177: More stretching. And I have an idea. I'll use Emma as a training aid. School is 1¼ miles away. We drive. From now on, we'll walk. We'll get fit together. She can sit on my stomach during sit-ups as well, as long as she promises not to jump up and down so much. I broach the idea. She likes the sit-ups bit but is less keen on the walking. Perhaps it's too far for a six-year-old. We try. She skips all the way there, leaving me wheezing halfway up Black Hill. I take the bus home.

I could improve my diet too, if I simply ate what I feed to my daughter. I could eat porridge, broccoli and carrots and tuna and apples and oranges each day. But I don't. I eat crumpets and cheese and pork pies. And biscuits.

Days 180–83: My month ends with two more rounds at Paxhill. Both are triumphs of sorts. The first makes me burst with pride, while the second – my debut in a club medal – makes me uneasy.

For the first round, James agrees to play. I warm up for forty-five minutes. James warms up with a strong coffee, a fag and a rich bout of coughing. My swing thought for the day comes from Hogan. I imagine a pane of glass leaning up from the ball to my shoulders. This will help my swing plane. I have a chipping thought – my forearms ahead of the ball at impact – and a putting thought – a forward press. James just hits.

The weather's gorgeous and I play phenomenally.

I score a Paxhill personal best of 12 over and, for the first time in the history of the universe, the galaxy and everything, I beat James. He scores 13 over. I keep a lid on things but inside I'm dancing a thousand jigs. I've beaten my mentor! I can barely believe it.

There's another landmark. James points it out.

I hit a surprisingly nice three-wood on the 10th.

'Shot,' James remarks.

'Thank you,' I reply.

'That's the first time you've ever done that,' James says.

'Hit a decent three-wood?'

'No, acknowledged a good shot. Normally, you say it was lucky, an accident or not what you intended.'

He's right. I apologise for good outcomes. Now I feel I half-deserve them. There's one thing, though, he says. We're playing off the yellows. 'In Saturday's medal, you'll be off the whites. That will be tougher.'

Nuts to white tees. I refuse to pay heed to such hair splitting. I continue my internal jigging. I began with a 24 handicap off the yellows and I've just hit 12 over off the yellows. I'm comparing like with like. I'm being consistent. I'm staying true to my yellow-teeness.

I feel like a fraud, entering the March medal. But it's the only way to get my handicap cut. Officially, I'm a 24 but I'm clearly better than that now. There've been no medals over the winter. Even if there had been, handicaps would not have been adjusted because of temporary greens.

So there's no way round it. I'll win and be branded a 'bandit', playing off a fictitiously high handicap. Bandit is a semi-affectionate word for a cheat. The only consolation, says James, is that I won't be alone.

'Bandits are everywhere. At least you have misgivings. Some people practise banditry throughout their golfing lives.'

I wash my clubs, shoes — and even clothes — the night before. It's a new theory. If I look good — notwithstanding the beard — perhaps I'll play well. I arrive early. The wind gets up.

My playing partner is called Gowdie and has the look of a bandit himself. He's off 27. He loves the game but rarely plays. On a good day he can play to 17, he says, and seems on course for that today. I progress nicely from tee to green but putt like a nonagenarian with Alzheimer's. When I miss a 2-footer Gowdie can't help intervening. Here I am, in the middle of my first medal, getting a lesson from a supposed inferior. Politely, I stick with my own method. I continue missing.

One thing I do learn from Gowdie, though. When he hits a green in regulation, he immediately starts discussing birdie chances. He's ultra positive. Self-doubt is simply not entertained. When I hit a green I hear the voice in my head say: 'With luck, you might just sneak a par here.'

Despite my putting, I scramble around in 17 over. Gowdie, meanwhile, gets his birdie but then inexplicably loses his head and plays to 25. I win the competition and I'm cut to 21.8. I still feel like a bandit, albeit a slightly less conspicuous one. Mission accomplished.

Emma is delighted with the medal and puts it in her jewellery box.

TWELVE
MIND GAMES

'All that we are is the result of what we have thought.
The mind is everything. What we think we become'

— Buddha

Weight: Frank and Clare's scales have packed up.
Waist measurement: Lost the tape measure.
Diet: I'm trying to introduce porridge.
Alcohol: Not telling.
Chronic Fatigue: Due to improve with the warmer weather?
Beard: Rasputin-esque.
Official handicap: 21.8
Rounds played: 16
Average score: 18.5 over
Average score over last ten rounds: 15.3 over
Average score over last five rounds: 16.4 over
Eagles: 0
Longest drive: 272 yards (16 March, Paxhill, 18th)
Number of range balls hit: 3,100
Self-belief: 7/10
And the secret of golf is . . . flexibility/touch your toes.

1 April, Day 184: 182 days – six months – to go.
Halfway. What have I achieved?

Officially, not a great deal. A handicap improvement of 2.2.

Unofficially, a fair bit. My average score over the last ten
rounds is 15.3 over – a drop of almost nine strokes.

Worryingly, though, last month's scores weren't too clever, with my last-five-round average increasing for the first time, from 14.2 to 16.4.

Now playing to around 15 or 16 sounds great. Absolutely great. When I started my year, I thought anything under 18 was useful. So why don't I feel better about it?

It's tough to answer. All I can say is that I still don't feel much of a player. Sure, I must have improved. But each time I reach Knightsbridge all I see is a video nasty. I've gone some way to taming my fundamental flaw – those rolling wrists – but only some of the way. Pharro wants me to concentrate on keeping my arms connected at the top of the backswing, and to get my shoulders turning further. I suppose I do hit straighter than I did. And longer. And yes, I've got a short game of sorts. I feel a little more flexible – I can almost touch Jan's toes now. But somehow it feels as if I've pulled off a neat trick to get this far, rather than changed things fundamentally.

Anyway. The next four weeks are all about abdominals, toe-touching and the short game. Ad nauseam.

I go to Paxhill and, for the very first time and on Malins' advice, I start with putting. Then I chip. Only then do I hit irons and woods. Normally I start – and end – with my driver. So simple. So obvious. So why have I never thought of it before?

I come home and do some sit-ups. Find one of Emma's birthday-party chocolate bars and put it back in the cupboard. Then take it out. Put it back in. Take it out. Eat it. Do some crunches, guiltily. Go shopping to replace the chocolate bar. But there's three in a packet. What shall I do with the other two?

178 days to go: Sit-ups, crunches, touch knees, eat second chocolate bar.

I head for a second lesson with Gilroy. I should have gone back before.

My stroke's still too long. I'm hitting more decisively, but there's still that 'post-impact acceleration'. And I'm too upright. Gilroy wants the top of my back and neck more horizontal.

175 days to go: We've got colds. Emma wakes up just before midnight. Jan's on an early shift so I take Emma into the spare room. She takes an hour to get back to sleep, then starts giving me a little kick every sixty seconds or so. Kick . . . kick . . . kick. I edge away. She follows. Kick . . . kick. I escape to the very edge of the bed. She follows. At 4 a.m. I have a brainwave. I sneak out of the bed and tiptoe round the other side. Within minutes Emma has turned around and . . . kick . . . kick . . . kick. I work it out at last. She's checking I'm still there. I take her to school with bags the size of Sussex under my eyes, feeling like the most important person in the world.

174 days to go: Crunches, sit-ups, stretch side and back muscles, flirt with shins, third chocolate bar. Then, without realising or even tasting, I eat Emma's replacement one as well. I'll buy some more.

I get my first text of the summer from the England and Wales Cricket Board. There's a press conference coming up. I won't be going, of course. I'm no longer a cricket journalist. I was, for years and years, but now I'm something else. Quite what I'm still not sure. My life, like my golf swing, is a work in progress.

But I still enjoy getting the texts. It makes me feel I'm still part of a loop. Odd, really. All I need to do is to phone up the England press officer and ask to be taken off the list. But I don't. When England tour the West Indies or India, I get the texts during the night as well, if I forget to turn off my mobile. I get woken up by the beep, discover that Kevin Pietersen is having a scan on a sore wrist, smile and go back to sleep. Don't ask me why, I just find it comforting. Odd, really.

169 days to go: I think it best to make things clear from the outset.

'I don't believe in you,' I venture after shaking Aaron Surtees' hand. 'Well, not you, as such. I mean I don't believe in hypnotherapy, or hypnotism, or whatever you call it.'

There's a pause. 'So why are you here?' he replies.

Good question. I'm not sure. Why exactly have I taken the 10.15 from Haywards Heath to London this morning? I spend the journey feeling self-conscious, to the point of avoiding eye contact with my fellow passengers. It must be written all over my face – I'm about to consult a hypnotherapist who'll somehow transform me into a better golfer. The words 'poppycock', 'pigs' and 'Heathrow Terminal 5' came to mind.

'I'm here on the off chance,' I reply.

On the off chance of what, though? On the off chance that I might be wrong in deriding sports psychology?

I'm decidedly old school on the subject. I'm pre-Victorian-children-up-chimneys. I maintain that you can either hack it or you can't. I'm not into the modern frilly stuff, where everybody empathises with the tortured £100,000-a-week footballer who misses a penalty. I liked it better when the tough got going even before the going got remotely tough.

I liked it when sportsmen didn't wear sarongs. I liked it when goalkeepers called Bert Trautmann soldiered on with broken necks in cup finals. Trautmann didn't appear in men's skin moisturiser ads. He appeared on the Russian Front as a paratrooper.

Did Rocky Marciano or All Black Colin Meads ever feel the need to lie on a psychiatrist's couch and discuss their traumatic childhoods? Did England fast bowler and former coal miner Harold Larwood worry about the niceties of Bodyline? I think not.

Sporting heroes shouldn't need pampering. If they get smacked in the mouth, they should swallow their teeth and shut up. Australian cricket all-rounder and World War II pilot Keith Miller summed it up best. When asked whether he, as an old timer, could begin to comprehend the massive mental pressures faced by modern-day sportsmen, he replied: 'I'll tell you what pressure is. Pressure is a Messerschmitt up your arse.'

I accept, albeit reluctantly, that there's a mental side to golf but even here I find myself at odds with the likes of Jack Nicklaus. Nicklaus says 90 per cent of the game is played in the mind. It may be for him. It's not for 24-handicappers. For us, it's 99.9 per cent about trying to ensure some sort of meaningful contact between the frigging bat and ball.

That said, my atheism has mellowed to agnosticism recently. An exchange with Malins prompts the rethink.

'How,' he asks, 'do you practise putting?'

'Without enthusiasm,' I say, adding that I usually concentrate, as per the golf magazines, on getting 20-footers to within dustbin-lid distance.

'How often do you hole those 20-foot putts?'

'Not very often. All right, never.'

'How often do you bother to hole out your second putt?'

'Er . . .'

'So your principal image is of the ball not going into the hole?' says Alastair, warming to his theme. 'In effect, you're practising to miss.'

'Er . . .'

In the past, I've blamed my putting mechanics. Post-Gilroy, though, that's less valid. I now understand what I'm trying to accomplish. I'm gaining in confidence, with my putts per round dropping from thirty-six to around thirty-two. But I know something's still not quite right. Perhaps I just need more time to practise the changes. Or could it really be that my mental approach is flawed?

That day, with Malins, I concentrate on holing out from 3, 4 and 5 feet. I begin to get used to the sound of a successful putt.

Malins notices something else.

'Are you aware, Tony, that your long putts all fall short?'

He's right. What's that all about? It's almost as if I'm afraid of what lies beyond the cup. 'Never up, never in', they say. Well, I'm rarely up and even more rarely anywhere in the vicinity of being in.

Perhaps – but please don't tell Trautmann, Marciano or Meads that I'm contemplating this – there really is something in this psychology lark after all.

When I tell James about Malins' observations, he tells me about Murat. Murat, a man with a smile imprinted into his genes, is the Paxhill bar manager. His son Emre is in Emma's school class. Murat is our version of Manuel The Waiter – I quote his wife Tracey on this – except that he's not a waiter, isn't stupid, doesn't have a moustache and hails from Turkey, not Barcelona. He's worked at the club for several years but appears to be allergic to golf. He's never been out on the course.

'Golf, eet's sillee,' says Murat.

He has, though, ventured on to the putting green, says James. And he holes everything. Absolutely everything.

'He hasn't got any baggage, you see. He doesn't understand that a 10-footer's difficult and a 5-footer nerve-racking. So he just holes them, time after time. "How do you do that?" I asked him once. "Eet's eezy. Just heet eet in the ole," he answered. If he ever takes up the game, he should never, ever have a putting lesson.' (Murat, I later discover, was a champion marksman during his national service in Turkey.)

A few days before my trip to see Surtees I run into neighbours Nicky and Frank. I casually slip my latest golf anecdote into the conversation, about how I'm afraid of golf holes. For once, they listen. Frank doesn't even yawn. The two, it transpires, are experts on self-help, psychology, positive thinking and hypnosis and NLP ...

'Neuro linguistic programming,' Frank explains. 'It's big in business management. It's all about positive mind-set and is based on studies of supremely successful people and the way they attain success.'

Nicky recounts how she used a self-hypnotism CD to stop buying junk food. 'That afternoon, I don't quite know how or why, I found myself chewing on broccoli stalks rather than munching through packs of crisps. It was weird.'

Before the day is out Andy, one house further down, chips in by lending me an NLP book. Everyone believes in this stuff, apparently.

I retreat to the computer and type 'NLP + golf'. Most of the search results come across as impenetrable jargon. One article on golf semantics, though, catches my eye.

Back in the midst of time, when a groat was worth a groat, drivers had been called 'play clubs'. That was what they were designed to do, after all – put the ball into play. But years later some clever marketing man – one of Mitch's forefathers, no doubt – had a brainwave and renamed them 'drivers'. It sounded sexier and far more macho.

The switch of vocabulary, the author argues, led to a switch in behaviour. Where once golfers had attempted to place their tee shots in the perfect position for their approaches, now, testosterone-crazed and clutching their new jumbo-headed clubs, they wound themselves up into paroxysms of delight and/or rage before attempting to smash the ball beyond Ursa Major. With, suffice to say, only moderate success.

It makes sense. I decide to re-christen my driver. It's my play club. My fairway finder.

Another Internet trawl and I find Aaron Surtees and City Hypnosis. On a whim, I phone up. On an even greater whim, he agrees to see me.

I indulge in some homework first.

Hypnotherapy claims to deal with the relationship between the conscious and unconscious mind. The conscious mind represents your critical faculty. While vital to day-to-day existence, it does prevent you from communicating with your subconscious mind. Whenever you feel something instinctively – one of those 'gut reactions' – your critical faculty tries to talk you out of it.

Hypnosis claims to disable it temporarily – a bit like turning off an over-vigilant computer firewall – thus allowing you to commune with your subconscious. Quite what that has to do with better golf I'm not sure. But what the heck. In for a penny, in for an Albanian Lek. I'll give it a whirl.

On meeting Surtees, I'm immediately on the defensive. He shares the building with yoga, Pilates, cranial massage, Tai Chi and stress management practitioners. There are groups of earnest-looking women in ethnic print, shadowed obediently by token, sallow, folk-singing men clutching leaflets about meditation and weekend retreats.

I feel horribly conspicuous until I find Surtees. Thank goodness – he's not wearing Indian-style robes and a turban, nor dancing around an incense stick. He's tall, pencil thin and immaculately suited, his manners as manicured as his nails. He talks softly, and with endearing hesitancy, as if he sees all three sides of the argument.

Surtees studied psychology without ever wanting to be a psychologist. Then a friend mentioned hypnotherapy and NLP. Within no time Surtees had set himself up in Harley Street, offering one-hour sessions to help people stop smoking.

'My first client was one of my girlfriend's work colleagues. Things went from there. It was mostly word of mouth,' he says.

Nowadays, he tackles issues ranging from fear of flying and public speaking to anger management, inadvertent blushing and any phobia you care to imagine. And some you don't. My favourite case involves a young woman who panicked whenever she approached an escalator. He's also helped sportsmen and women, including a golfer who played well on the range but fell apart on the course.

'I think hypnotherapy will be huge in sport,' Surtees tells me. 'It already is in the US. If you're looking for a secret, this may be it. People ask why leading sportsmen need help. Well, they have their games checked out by technical coaches, so why not a mental coach? A lot of sportsmen know they can scale certain heights but fail to do so consistently. That can have something to do with mental make-up. Not that everybody needs it. I don't suppose Muhammad Ali ever had a mental coach.'

My point exactly! Let's be honest, Aaron, this is all cleverly marketed twaddle to pamper the weak-willed . . .

But Surtees reckons he enjoys a 70–80 per cent success rate.

So what exactly is hypnotism, and NLP? How does it work? And why's it needed?

Surtees hesitates. He's not, he says, interested in hypnoanalysis, which seeks to unearth the origins of a phobia. Hypnotherapy is more direct.

'Think of people's insecurities as computer short-circuits. They seem to occur randomly, and often very suddenly. One woman came to me petrified of driving. She was on the motorway one rainy night and got beeped at. She had a panic attack and felt she couldn't turn the steering wheel. Another person got the same reaction after walking into a crowded room. It happens to people in all walks of life, although I get a large number of young professionals, many in finance jobs struggling to live up to expectations.'

As for hypnosis, well, 'there's no set, magical hypnotic state. It varies from person to person. The Greek word means "sleep like". People drift in and out of this state but are perfectly capable of hearing. In a way, it's a heightened state of consciousness. You relax, you drift, and you're susceptible to suggestion.

'I try to switch negatives into positives. A particular experience has often become associated with something bad, as in the case of the car driver. She'd previously enjoyed driving, so it was a case of re-establishing it with a positive emotion, of breaking down mental barriers through a variety of techniques like visualisation.

'Each story is unique. All I'm doing is helping people help themselves. You could call it a trick of the mind. To set things straight.'

Some people, of course, don't buy into it. 'That's not ideal. But it doesn't mean we can't achieve results.' Take the woman and the escalators. She was a journalist and later wrote an article on the experience. 'She was analysing everything I was saying and felt awake throughout. She felt in control and wrote that she wouldn't have barked like a dog or clucked like a chicken if I'd suggested it. But within a day she was back on escalators. It shows that being hypnotised is different for everyone. Other people can't remember a thing afterwards.'

It's my turn on the couch. Actually, it's a comfortable, deep, black leather chair.

My main problem, I say, lies with my putting. It's a half-truth. It used to be the case. But I want to try hypnotism, so I need a problem. I'm not fantastic at putting, but then I'm not fantastic at anything. I could say my driving's erratic. But putting seems the better idea. It's more of a mind game. And I am undeniably negative as soon as I spy a green.

My putting's expressed in 'don'ts'. 'Don't three-putt. Don't screw it up. Don't forget to allow for the slope. Don't forget to clean the putter-head . . .'

It takes me back to a book we bought when Emma was born; *The Secret of Happy Children*, it was called. Kids, ridiculously, don't come with user manuals. It's something I've often complained about. Anyway, one section dealt with positive ways of addressing children. Most parents say: 'Don't fall out of the tree.' Few opt for: 'Hold on to the branch carefully.' It's not altogether surprising that our kids grow up with dents in their foreheads.

'Oh, and one last thing,' I add, trying to make it sound as an afterthought. I pause, half-wishing that I'd not spoken. But I'm in confessional mode.

'It's just that . . . '

Surtees looks concerned. Perhaps he thinks I'm about to confess to some disgusting social habit, or that I'm from the Inland Revenue.

'It's just that there are two people in my head. There's me, and there's this second voice – I've christened it Old Tom Morris – which is forever giving me technical advice and reminding me of my swing faults and warning me about this danger or that. It's always with me during a round and gets particularly vocal when I putt. I know it sounds mad . . .'

Surtees smiles. 'There are two voices in a lot of people's heads,' he says. The key, apparently, is not to allow Old Tom to commentate on my game, particularly when I'm playing poorly. I should try to distract him or divert his attention on to a specific subject, like the rhythm of my swing. That may stop him acting as my judge and jury all the time.

We begin. I lie back, shut my eyes and think of Paxhill.

I am not sure how to describe what follows. Let's just say it's odd. I, like Escalator Lady, am convinced I can remember everything he says. At no stage do I cluck or bark. But I certainly relax. Indeed, I find the whole thing hugely enjoy-able. I sink so deep into Surtees' magic chair that I doubt I'll ever manage to clamber back out. But I don't feel I entered a hypnotic state and I tell Surtees so afterwards.

'That happens,' he says. 'How long do you think the session lasted?'

I think about ten minutes, so I say fifteen. 'It was forty,' he replies.

That's odd. Seriously odd. Perhaps one's time-keeping suffers behind closed eyelids.

Walking to the Tube, I write down everything he said, to prove that I was conscious.

'First,' I scribble on the back of my train timetable, 'he told me to relax.' I was at level one and that descended to two, three, four and five. There was something about steps leading down into a sunny garden. My face and wrists would begin to feel warm (that had been strange – seconds before, I'd felt a burning sensation on my right wrist). Then there'd been something about my left arm being lifted into the air by an imaginary helium balloon.

'Finally he began talking about golf. I was putting. Then he said . . . '

As I walk along, I feel this overwhelming urge to putt. I spot a lamp post, bin or drainpipe, stop, line up and try to sense the weight of putt required. I home in on a new target. A woman walks out of a shop and we collide as I'm assessing a 10-footer, with a little left-to-right break between a Mars wrapper and a crate of milk bottles. She stares at me, petrified.

Now then, let's see, Surtees also said something about . . .

But my recollection of the session is fading. I grab at the nearest memory but it flies beyond my reach, like a loose newspaper sheet caught in a spiralling gust of wind. With each step that I take, the less I remember. The harder I try, the blanker my mind becomes. Soon, I can't remember a thing. I'm erased.

Now I'm not saying I'm converted. I'm just intrigued. Where did that missing half-an-hour go, for a start? And how on earth have I forgotten what Surtees was saying, barely twenty minutes ago? It's bizarre.

Not half as bizarre, though, as what happens a couple of days later.

167 days to go: Surtees said I should play as soon as possible, so Friday's booked. James is away. I'm on my own.

Crunches. Sit-ups. Stretches. Practise pointing my thumb at my nose.

I decide to shave off my beard. Jan stopped kissing weeks ago and Emma's now joined the boycott. And I think I frightened Surtees a bit with the Wild Man of Borneo look. Holly, Tarin and Libby have also been looking a bit concerned in the school playground. And anyway, it's becoming a distraction. I keep chewing at it.

It takes me forty minutes.

'Daddy, it's you!' says Emma. 'You're back!'

166 days to go: I drive to the club and I feel, well . . . unusual. Unusual as in supremely confident. Not something I indulge in too often. I just know I'm going to break 10 over today, for the first time in my life. I don't think, I know.

Old Tom snorts derisively. 'Look at your last six or seven rounds,' he reminds me. 'Not exactly inspirational. And you haven't played for a while . . . ' He has a point, albeit a negative one. I do not extend him the courtesy of a reply.

I just know. Is it to do with Surtees? Who knows? But it's not that hard, if you think about it. All I need are five pars on each nine. I can even afford one double bogey.

I warm up. It's not as if I'm draining all my putts, but nothing, absolutely nothing, ends up short. First blood to Surtees. Old Tom goes quiet.

10.15 a.m. Four-and-a-half hours to Emma. Yellow tees. Let's go.

1st hole: 370-yard par four. Tough hole. A bogey's fine. I'm never sure. Driver – sorry, 'play club' – or three-wood? There are two fairway bunkers, the second 220-odd yards away. But the wind's with. Play club. I smash as good an opening shot as I'll ever strike. It runs out to 260 yards. I hit a wedge to 15 feet. Two putts. Par. Wow.

2nd: 162-yard uphill par three. Again, a bogey's good. Two old timers, dawdling by the tee, wave me through. 'You don't like audiences,' chuckles Old Tom. On a cold day it's a four-iron. Today? Downwind . . . could it be a six? But anything short runs off into the left-hand bunker. I take the five and laser a one-in-a-hundred shot to the back fringe. The old timers are impressed. Me too. I try to behave as if it's an everyday thing. I fat my chip to 8 feet but ram home the putt. Par. Wow. Wow.

3rd: 472-yard par five. Straightforward, downhill, bunker-less. Small pond near the green. I fade-slice but get decent distance. I'm a rescue club away but the pond's directly in my line. Be conservative. I hit a nice six, then bump-and-run an eight-iron to a foot. One putt. Birdie! Wow. Wow. Wow.

4th: 308-yard par four. Easy hole. Short and straight, two bunkers defending a two-tier green. My drive's solid but cuts right. I pull a half-shot with my 52-degree wedge to 15 feet.

Two putts. Heck and wow. I've never started this well. Keep calm now.

5th: 118-yard par three. Short, uphill and blind to a small, undulating green with a bunker across the front. My eight-iron draws over the flag but lands long. I hit it too well! I chip back 4 feet past. I hole out again. I'm wowed out. Gilroy and Surtees won't believe this . . .

6th: 479-yard downhill par five. Fairway bunker. I opt for safety and hit an average three-iron. I then thin a four-iron but it runs for ever, leaving 80 yards. I skull my wedge to the back fringe, putt back and leave a knee-knocking 5-footer. I sink it. Miraculous. Especially since I didn't hit a single good shot . . .

'Go through your seventeen current swing drills and find out why,' suggests Old Tom. Ignore him.

7th: 396-yard uphill par four. Stroke index one. Certain bogey. A small green, with front bunkers and a bank of snarled rough at the back. I aim left, drive right, to about 240 yards, then block a lucky five-iron past the bunkers. I'm 15 feet short of the green. I chip a nine-iron dead. Par. On the 7th! Keep very, very calm.

8th: 373-yard downhill par four. A perfect driving hole. I cut into the light rough. 130 yards to the flag. I go for a nine-iron instead of my pitching-wedge and bounce long, but short of the back bunker. I chip back up to 4 feet. Par.

And then, suddenly, it dawns on me. Heck . . . I'm 1 under!

The golf books say never get ahead of yourself, and never

dwell on the past either. Tiger Woods, apparently, has a 30-yard rule after bad shots. He can fume for those 30 yards, but then he must move on. Nice idea – but what if your bad shots go only 25 yards? I rarely get ahead of myself anyway. I normally lag way behind. But today's not normal. Today's paranormal.

The books also tell you not to add up your score during a round. Play each hole as it comes. But how could I not know the score this time? Some people, apparently, can't handle success and subconsciously sabotage themselves. I'm not afraid of succeeding. I'm afraid of believing. I feel as if I've woken from a gorgeous dream to find it's really happening. That's truly tough to take.

9th: 348-yard par four. I fight the urge to text Roger. I'm in a state of over-excitement. I'm hyperventilating. It's that or hay fever. Dogleg left, uphill. Out of bounds on both sides. I slice badly but I don't think it's OB. I slice my provisional as well.

My luck runs out. I tread on three balls in the rough, but not mine. I play the provisional, cut my approach right but get up and down. Double bogey. Damnation. That was a second-ball par . . . The ifs and buts begin. 'Why are you hitting everything to the right all of a sudden?' asks Old Tom.

10th: 302-yard par four. The first of three holes with out of bounds right. I top my three-wood 50 yards. With that, the spell's broken. I rush my next and pull it behind a tree. I chip sideways with my third. The bunker's still in line. Sod it. But I pitch close and get up and down. 'What a fiasco,' says Old Tom. He wants to discuss the drive.

11th: 257-yard par four. A blind tee shot, dropping down to a green guarded by bunkers. OK five-iron. A short pitch but my ball trickles off the back. Chip dead with a nine-iron. Back on track.

12th: Nasty downhill 209-yard par three. Out of bounds right, grass bank left. Three-wood's too long, three-iron too short. Inexplicably, I go for a five. I pull into the rough. My head's addling, I'm unravelling. Somehow I gouge the ball out and it rolls to 3 feet. Brilliant! The putt lips out. Blast!

13th: 302-yard par four, dogleg right. Just cut a three-wood or rescue club around the trees. But when I try to fade I always pull. So I aim straight. A perfect fade. 52-degree wedge to 15 feet. Par. Deep breath. Regroup.

14th: Tough 396-yard uphill par four. Stroke index two. Fairway bunker 200 yards on the left. I hit a belter, straight out to 240 yards. Six-iron, aimed a tad left but it fails to fade. Chip to 5 feet. Miss the putt. I'll take that.

15th: 472-yard par five. Downhill drive, ditch and trees right. Aim at the left-hand fairway bunker. I change my mind mid-swing and go for the middle. Slice into the trees. Slice provisional into trees. Second provisional. A nice three-iron.

So that's it. Thrown away. Just like that. What a waste. 'Clown,' comments Old Tom. I'm set to play the second provisional when, on a hunch, I cut through the trees. My first two balls have cleared them and are sitting next to the 14th fairway! Semi-delirious, I chunk my first ball into more trees, take a drop, hit short of the green, pitch to 8 feet and two-putt. A good double bogey if ever there was one.

16th: 159-yard par three. I steal a look at my scorecard. I need one par and two bogeys for 9 over. Fine. The 16th's OK, 17th's easy, 18th's tough. Go for it. I pull a six-iron into the rough, scuff out to 10 feet, miss the putt. Pity.

17th: 312-yard par four. The moment of truth. I aim left but cut right. 64 yards to carry the greenside bunker. Good. My lob-wedge bounces off the green. Bad. Poor chip. Another 10-foot putt. I haven't left anything short all day. Nice strike. Right on line . . . one roll shy. Bogey. Disastrous.

18th: 397-yard par four. I feel suddenly exhausted and top my drive 70 yards. The recriminations begin. 1 under after eight and now this. OK-ish three-wood. 115 yards to go, over a pond and trees. Wait a minute, though – I can still do this! An up and down will do!

It's a good lie but I'm between clubs. It's a phenomenal wedge or an average nine. I take a deep breath, visualise and hit a phenomenal wedge. So phenomenal that it runs off the back. I chip to 5 feet, then, from somewhere, summon the pride to take the putt seriously. It drops. Bogey. Ten over. My best ever, but not good enough. To quote Hugh Grant: 'Fuck. Fuck. Fuck.'

I sit in the corner of the bar, staring morosely at the floor. After five minutes I get out my scorecard, albeit reluctantly, and sift through the wreckage.

'So where did it go wrong?' says Old Tom, eager for the post-mortem.

You don't need to be Sherlock Holmes. A classic case of mental meltdown. I couldn't handle success, after all. As for the details, well, I hit six out of fourteen fairways, leaving most of my approaches coming from the rough. Result? Only four greens in regulation. Include two duffed tee shots and it's a miracle that I've even played to 10.

I rally. There were some positives. A few of my irons were simply too good. They were so well struck that they missed long. That's a new problem. And what about my putting! No threes. I tot them up. Strewth – twenty-six putts! That's European Tour! My best number ever, by four! Two days after being hypnotised and a week after a putting lesson! And eleven out of thirteen chips to within 8 feet is good, too.

Murat comes over.

'Another beeer, Tonee? How dju play? U aven't added up your back nine yet. Let meee seee . . . '

I am about to say 'no thanks, I'd better not, I'm driving' and '10 over, dammit' but Murat's too quick. So I look out of the window, then look up, and Murat says . . .

'Hey, dju donit, Tonee. Dju donit!'

'Donut,' I tell him. 'It's: "You donut, Tony".'

'No, dju donit – 9 over!'

I rip the card back. I recount. My God. I thought I'd double-bogeyed the 10th. It felt like a double but no, I got up and down. He's right! My God. Wait a minute . . . wait . . . I really have donit! I've played to a single figure-handicap! I've played to 9 over! I'm a golfer! My quest is over, with five months to spare. Finito. Basta. Bloody brilliant!

James should have been here. Half of this is down to him. I text Jan, in capitals.

'I'VE DONE IT!!!'

Then I text Niall (I don't text James. He's still hasn't got the hang of his mobile phone yet).

Jan texts back. 'Done what?'

Niall texts back. 'Swam without armbands?'

Murat wanders off. I celebrate alone.

164 days to go: For the next three days, I don't touch a club. I just bask in glory. Jan's at her wits' end. She's heard about my drive on the 1st, my chip on the 3rd and that final putt about 1,675 times (her estimation, not mine. And is that 1,675 descriptions of each shot or 1,675 in total? If it's the latter – making it 558.33 recurring descriptions per shot – I don't see why she's complaining).

Frank, meanwhile, has heard my hole-by-hole résumé only once – admittedly a protracted once, while he was watching *Match of the Day*, but only once nevertheless. You'd think he could afford me another audience. But Clare says he's been unexpectedly called away to Patagonia on business.

It's his loss.

So now what? A second round in singles is a formality. I've broken the mental barrier. I'll probably do it next time out.

THIRTEEN

THE GREAT GOLF CONSPIRACY

'People of the same trade seldom meet together, even for merriment and diversion, but the conversation ends in a conspiracy against the public'

— *George Adam Smith*

Weight/waist/diet/alcohol: No longer up for discussion. A private matter.

Chronic Fatigue: One hour a day. Try to nap through lunch hour and kill two birds with one stone?

Beard: Gone.

Official handicap: 21.8

Rounds: 17

Average score: 17.94

Average score over last ten rounds: 14.8

Average score over last five rounds: 14.4

Eagles: 0

Longest drive: 272 yards (16 March, Paxhill, 18th)

Range balls: 3,400

Self-belief: 10/10

And the secret of golf is . . . hypnotism. And shaving off beards.

1 May, Day 214: 151 to go.

'So nobody actually witnessed this single-figure round of yours, then?' says James. 'In which case it can hardly be called official, can it?'

He looks deadpan, I downcast. Then he smiles and shakes my hand.

My elation, however, is short-lived. James is leaving. He'll be gone in a couple of weeks. Paxhill will also be gone. It will become Lindfield Golf Course, housing a college of aspiring, teenage would-be professionals. From plebeian Paxhill to lofty Lindfield. There's no room for James under the new management. There'll be no room for Tweedle Dums and Tweedle Dees. Everyone will wear Pringle. I'll be the only one eating them. So there'll probably be no room for me either.

150 days to go: I console myself with the thought that my challenge is suddenly going far, far better than expected. Seven months gone, a putting guru, a physiotherapist and a hypnotist behind me and I'm already as good as home. Even with the breaking of two toes. One more round of singles, then beat my brothers and I'm there. Piece of cake.

It's only 9 a.m. but I eat one — a rather large piece — in celebration of my achievement.

And I console myself with the 1,827 leaflets I picked up at last month's London Golf Show. I spread them out and gawp like a child with its head jammed inside a sweet jar. I gorge on glossy photographs of oversized drivers, alignment aids and swing guides, I feast on graphite and titanium. I delight in the possibilities. I want them all and I want them now. Everything is very shiny, very packaged and utterly revolutionary. They come in all sizes and guises. They all have unique secrets to divulge. They are all, apparently, absolutely fundamental to good golf.

Like a glutton stuffed full with over-egged promises, though, I start feeling sick.

Something's not quite right. Something doesn't ring true.

I've always fondly imagined the golf industry on my side. They want me to improve. They want me happy. It's their fundamental mission, surely? But what if they were really more interested in my money than my handicap?

Can there really be so many so-very-vital products? Can there be so many secrets? Could I be the victim of some great conspiracy?

That evening, I watch a golf advertisement featuring John Daly. Daly's a favourite of mine. He's advertising a driver. You see him on the putting green but he gets bored. You see him in a bunker, but that's not for him either. No, says Big John, golf's all about your driver. 'You can lower your score when you hit it long,' he announces.

I laugh. The ad's pure Mitch. Then I stop.

I'm not saying it's dishonest. But it's not the whole truth. Everyone knows that Daly, despite being a gargantuan hitter, also has exquisite touch. The man's not mere beef and blitz. But that's the caricature on sale here. 'Don't worry about such irrelevancies as direction' seems to be the subliminal message. 'Just belt the life out of it.'

Now I'm offended. Big John's better than that. I turn off the TV and resort to a book; *The Hungry Years – Confessions of a Food Addict*, by William Leith. It's fun. It's not helping me curb my over-eating but it makes me laugh. I read happily away. Until I come to a section on snacking.

Leith doesn't like snacks. They are, he writes, an advertisement for themselves. They miss the point. 'The products that do well are the ones that do not satisfy. The ideal product is addictive,' he argues. 'Americans spend $32 million on snacks per year. You eat one, and you want another one. Eat. Want. A vicious circle. Unless you are a manufacturer.'

My God! The same applies to golf! In America, I've read, around $5 billion a year is spent on the sport. Buy. Want. Buy. Want. But nobody gets any better. It's a vicious circle. Unless you are a manufacturer.

Perhaps they don't want me happy, they want me hungry! Perhaps I'm being fed junk.

14.8 days to go: I stay home. I don't even swing my clubs. Why? Is it a sense of anticlimax? Am I golfed-out? Or am I fearful that the magic might vanish? I choose to do the ironing instead, and make a pork casserole, which is odd. Jan eats it without complaining, which is odder still. I teach Emma how to stand up in the saddle while riding her bike. We play catch. Emma is as sporty as her mother. She couldn't catch a cold.

14.6 days to go: James is packed. For old time's sake, he invites me to join his team in a charity Stableford event. Summer arrives overnight. I've played almost all my golf with James and I want to show him how much he's helped.

But I don't. I play OK, to 14, but without suggesting that I can play to singles. I don't own the golf swing after all. I've just borrowed it, on the shortest of loans.

Two of my shots stand out – one appalling drive and one fantastic one. The appalling, from the 3rd tee, slices so wildly that it flies across the adjoining 4th fairway and lands on the 6th. The fantastic, on the 18th, causes jubilation among our team. There's a long-drive competition. I've hit the ball as well as I can and it surpasses the existing marker by 30 yards. When we get there, though, we find it's the ladies' marker. I've driven 277 wonderful yards but the men's best stands at 304.

Our team doesn't win a thing. But at least I'm the ladies' long drive champion.

Afterwards, I tell James about the Golf Show and of my suspicions about being sold short.

James, to my surprise, agrees. And he tells me a story.

Some years back, a leading manufacturer launched a set of irons, marketing them as a major advance in design and technology. They promised extra distance. Don't they always?

But this time they delivered. People who hit seven-irons 140 yards now hit 150. Golf's version of the Gold Rush ensued. Everybody bought the clubs, everybody was delighted and they all marched happily off into the sunset.

Or rather, they didn't. Because handicaps still didn't go down. And there was another downside. People mysteriously found their new two- and three-irons harder to hit and eventually consigned them to the garage. Also, there was now a bigger distance gap between their new nine-iron and old pitching-wedge. Our resourceful manufacturers, however, solved the conundrum by launching a series of 'gap-wedges'. Cue second Gold Rush.

So what was the secret of the magic clubs?

'All that had happened,' says James, 'is that they'd tweaked the lofts. They strengthened their seven-irons into sixes, while continuing to call them sevens. In the 1960s, a six-iron had 36 degrees of loft and a seven 40. Today, a seven has about 34–35 degrees. Today's seven is, in effect, yesterday's five-and-a-half. Today's wedge is yesterday's nine. There's no industry standard, you see – they can write any number they want on a clubhead.

'It didn't help us play better. But it helped them sell a lot more clubs.'

I shake my head. Then I shake James's hand. I hope he finds time to drop in at Paxhill – sorry, Lindfield – from time to time.

139 days to go: When Emma was born I vowed, in my wonderment, that I'd never get angry with her and never raise my voice, whatever the provocation.

Today I blow it.

I've been trying to teach Emma how to read the time. She doesn't get it. In retrospect, it's hardly surprising. Five minutes, ten, fifteen, none mean anything to her. She thrives in the here-and-now. She doesn't get it, she doesn't mind, and, wonderfully carefree, she laughs.

I do mind, though. I mind that I'm not clever enough to make her see. I hear myself bark: 'Why won't you concentrate, just for a second? How can anyone be so stupid!'

I want to swallow the words right back down, but it's too late. I've suggested my precious little daughter, bright as a button, sharp as a tack, sensitive as May flowers, is as dull as ditch water. There are uncomprehending tears in her eyes.

'Please don't speak to me in capital letters, Daddy,' she says.

She doesn't understand where her loving dad has gone to all of a sudden.

I send myself to the naughty step, where I ask the same question. As a child, teenager and adult I pushed myself hard. And where did it get me? Rapidly heading for my half-century, having lived my life according to Protestant work ethics, I am beaten and battered, exhausted and ill. I burnt myself out. And for what? Nothing of much importance, I'd say. I feel ashamed. For no good reason, I've got angry with my gorgeous little girl. Perhaps I'm just angry with the way I've lived my own life.

Later, I tell Jan. She's understanding. It's not easy being a parent, everyone has bad days, mistakes are allowed. She forgives me. I'm not sure I do. I wince. For weeks.

I give Emma lots of chocolate over the next few days, in an attempt to buy forgiveness. Within hours of my outburst she already has no idea what there is to forgive, but she accepts the chocolate. She'll go far. Either that or get very fat.

137 days to go: Sit-ups. Go for my toes and touch my shins. Funny time to buy new clubs, just as I'm losing faith in the industry. But I haven't lost faith in everyone. Not in individuals, just big business. James always said clubs could make a difference, particularly to poorer players.

Personally, I've always sided with Robert Browning when he wrote: 'The trouble that most of us find with the modern matched sets of clubs is that they don't really seem to know any more about the game than the old ones did.' But among my Golf Show leaflets there's one for Precision Golf, a two-man band specialising in personalised club fitting. I call.

135 days to go: Lesson with Pharro.

'Hugh?'

'No.'

We refine my takeaway and turn. I'm getting closer, he says.

'It's just the wrists — your killer flaw — that we need to work on a bit, Lord Antony. Then we'll concentrate on the top of the backswing. You're lifting with your arms rather than turning your shoulders and torso.'

I'm a bit down. I share my doubts with Pharro. I'm even

beginning to question the teaching. Are teachers really getting through to their pupils? I'm not even sure they understand the problems of the average hacker. How can they? They've played flawless golf from the cradle. Those who can't do, teach, so the adage goes. In golf, it's the other way round but I'm not sure that's necessarily any better.

And what about half-hour lessons? We get shown something, we have a few goes and then we go away and almost immediately start doing it wrong again. We're not supervised. When you learn to drive a car, you're monitored between lessons. Even if it is by your aunt Maisie, the one with the bifocals who caused those infamous pile-ups on the M62. Golf lessons are a bit like showing children how to strike matches, before telling them to go and practise on their own in a field of haystacks.

Pharro, to my surprise, laughs.

'There's plenty of bad learning going on and plenty of bad teaching,' he says. 'I'm not rubbishing my own trade but the key to teaching is to make your student understand why he hits good or bad shots. That's not happening enough. A lot of places, like driving ranges, churn people through lessons without building relationships.

'Look, golf teachers are always changing jobs. So here's a question. How many clients do they take with them? I guarantee that only about 1 per cent keep all their clients. Ten per cent may keep one or two. The vast majority move on empty handed.

'People who can swing aren't necessarily the right people to teach. And good teaching's the key to good learning.'

Pharro illustrates his own story. Like the rest, he tried to become a professional player. He played as a kid, took it seriously from the age of twelve and was scratch by fifteen. He played amateur county golf, then turned pro and tried to make a living. He worked as a waiter at weekends to fund his golf on the mini tours. He gave himself three years. It didn't work out.

When Knightsbridge Golf School offered him work, he jumped at the chance.

'I wasn't a natural teacher at first. When you turn pro you say you'll never teach – that would be like predicting your own failure. But I love it now. I don't consider that I failed. I tried, and if you try you never fail. I reckon 70 per cent of teaching is enthusiasm.'

Learners must accept that they're in golf for the long haul, he says. It's a marathon. They also have to try to avoid confusion.

'In America, they reckon there's about fifty official golf teaching methods. There's always someone with a new idea. But I reckon there's only one secret.

'Hit the ball straight. If your club's square to the target at impact it's going to go straight. If your clubface is square to your body throughout the swing, the ball goes straight. That's what we teach. It's that simple.'

134 days to go: I go out on my own, in glorious weather, and go round in 16 over par. I don't hit straight. I hit huge, horrible, depressing hooks. How the hell did I ever manage to go round in 9 over? Perhaps I dreamt it.

132 days to go: I'm back in the local swimming pool with Roy and our hysterical, E-numbered daughters. Hippo One meets Hippo Two. I rant about golf companies and teachers, water bubbles foaming rabidly at the corners of my mouth.

'That's today's society,' replies Roy. 'Everybody wants a three-minute fix. Everybody wants to learn how to play the piano without bothering with scales. That's why gyms have big recruiting drives in March. By then, 90 per cent of New Year resolutions have worn off and people are back in the pub with the pork scratchings.

'But industries just give people what they want. You can't blame them. They're catering for a need. It's not up to industry to decide whether that need's appropriate. People dream, companies provide. Is it McDonald's fault that you like eating burgers and chips? Humans are the problem. Humans and human failings are the cause of high handicaps.'

Spoken like a true business manager. Remind me never to buy anything off this man.

I'm still unsure. I feel golf is a game half lost in translation and half lost in deception. But Roy's delighted with the neatness of his analysis. He grunts and declines the opportunity of further debate by submerging into the deep end.

131 days to go: Summer lasts an apologetic eight and three-quarter days. May turns out to be December. There are hail stones on the greens.

I drive up to Surrey and Precision Golf. I feel like a phoney – most of their clients are single handicappers at worst, professionals at best – but, at the same time, I secretly hope for a miracle.

James used to say that bad swing mechanics will always overcome good technology. But he also maintained that fitted clubs could make a difference. I know that new clubs won't sort out my unreliable wrists. But I'm hoping they might be more understanding of my foibles.

I bought my clubs years ago. I liked the second-hand price, had a brisk swish and I paid. Hopefully I'll now discover that they are singularly ill-suited. They've been designed for a towering Miss Universe with a thunderous 120mph golf swing, rather than a muscle-less, 5ft 8½in sedentary 49-year-old dough ball with a 12mph slap. I pray that the guys at Precision will nod knowingly after my very first swing – 'can you believe it, he's still managed to improve with those clubs!' – and thrust a killer iron or driver into my hand.

James Davey and Simon Cooper seem to have all the bases covered. Davey is dark, short, quiet and studious. He makes. Cooper is tall, blond, outgoing and loquacious. An ex-player, he fits. They're independent, too, which is rare. They have an independent, computerised database of components, allowing them to provide almost any combination of clubhead, shaft and grip.

The first job is to look at my clubs and my swing.

Cooper asks if I play other sports? Do I hit high or low? Do I take divots? What's my bad shot? 'The next one,' I answer. He warns from the outset. 'If I think the problem is your swing rather than the clubs, I'll tell you. You have to be realistic with what you can achieve with new equipment.'

Damn. He's on to me already.

I'm analysed on Flightscope, a launch monitor which spews out reams of data on ball flight, spin, swing speed and clubhead path. My clubhead lie angle is checked. My shafts are examined for irregularities which may cause bending or twisting. 'The nearest analogy is balancing a car tyre,' says Cooper.

I just about understand. I've a vague idea what swing weight means, and torque, flex and lie. I abide by the Chinese proverb 'he who asks is a fool for a moment, he who does not is a fool for ever'. I ask a lot of questions.

There's some good news. My swing, says Cooper, isn't bad. My set up's neutral, my timing's nice and I make a heavy, connected sound at impact. I'm going through the ball at around 80mph. Something about me reminds him of David Duval. Is that early, Open-winning Duval or late, missed-the-cut-again Duval?

'You clear nicely with the body. Everything's together. It's through a strong base. It looks a smooth action but there's more strength there than with people who swing harder.'

There's even time for a tip. He thinks I'm gripping too hard. I should free-wheel.

I tell him I prefer my irons. My woods tend towards the haphazard. I occasionally hit belters but, overall, they go here, there, everywhere.

He nods. The iron heads, Cooper says, are fine. But the steel shafts are heavy – among the heaviest around, in fact. They play firm. The woods' shafts are a lot softer, which means I overload them and get dangerous head twist through impact.

'Your three-wood's the worst, it's probably a "shit-or-bust" club. When you get it right, I bet it goes miles, with a late whip. But get it wrong . . . '

Cooper swings my driver. He looks like Ernie Els of course. Bastard. The Flightscope records 308 yards. Bastard bastard. Cooper, though, like Pharro, did not make it as a player. His hopes of a professional career were undermined by ill health. He played a year on the EuroPro Tour. 'I played solidly rather than fantastically. I did all the right things, in terms of fitness and nutrition. I even saw a life coach. But I ran myself into the ground physically.

'I put too much stress on myself, and there was an element of paralysis by analysis, which isn't great when you're trying to make a living. I've always been good on theory, even if it didn't help my playing. I wanted to know how things worked.'

That curiosity was a bonus when Davey suggested a partnership.

Cooper was still good enough to reach the 2006 Open final qualifying. 'I know I can play some very nice golf but it's about consistency. There are so many good players. Quite a few don't hit as well as I do, but there's more to it than that, like the way you manage yourself. In my heart of hearts, I know I'm not quite good enough. I can live with that.'

I ask about average handicaps and the industry. Cooper and Davey are refreshingly frank.

'It's interesting,' says Cooper. 'In theory, people should have got better but it's a sport with so many variables. I wonder whether it's easier to get things wrong today because there are so many options. Look at all the swing theories.

'As for the industry not helping you, well, why would it want to? Manufacturers don't want you to have the best clubs. They want you to have their latest model.

'And as for club fitting, more people offer it nowadays, but it's not exactly thorough. In golf shops, assistants measure you from wrist to floor, offer you three clubs to try, then sell you the one you prefer. It's not exactly exhaustive or scientific. We don't call that club fitting.'

Davey argues that mass-produced clubs aren't built to last, 'they don't want you to have something to keep'. He confirms James's story about 'vanishing lofts', then adds a twist.

Today's drivers, he says, have also been tweaked, but in the opposite direction. 'Most golfers want to hit 8.5-degree drivers because it sounds macho. But the manufacturers know that the average golfer can't hit them. They would worm-burn. So they sell drivers with 8.5 stamped on the head when, in fact, the club has been set to 10 degrees to ensure the ball gets airborne.'

Cooper thinks new clubs could save me up to five shots, mainly because of my erratic woods. We also decide to swap my three-iron for a rescue.

The clubs will be ready in a matter of weeks. Five shots? I sign on the dotted line.

121 days to go: I've squeezed in a few lessons over the last week – putting with Gilroy ('too upright again'); pitching with Malins ('your club's closed on the takeaway, you're sitting back on your right foot and flicking your hands'); and the full swing with Pharro ('try to get the feel of throwing your arms and hands down the target line').

I return to Paxhill/Lindfield with borrowed clubs and go round in 16 over. Again. Irritating. I pull a few shots and duff a bunch of chips from messy lies. Pulling is becoming an issue. I want a repeatable swing, dammit. A repeatable straight swing, that is.

It's not been a great month. It feels like two steps forward and three back. Four months left. I've done the putting, the chipping, the pitching, the physio, the hypnotism and the new clubs and I seem to be going in the wrong direction. What's next?

FOURTEEN
THE MAN IN THE WHITE COAT

'I hear and I forget. I see and I remember. I do and I understand.'

— *Chinese proverb*

Weight: OK, I admit it – I haven't lost any.
Waist: No thinner.
Diet: Still rubbish.
Alcohol: Still excessive.
Chronic Fatigue: Good.
Official handicap: 21.8
Rounds: 20
Average score: 17.55 over
Average score over last ten rounds: 14.9 over
Average score over last five rounds: 14.4 over
Eagles: 0
Longest drive: 277 yards (6 May, Lindfield, 18th – Ladies' Long Drive Champion)
Number of range balls hit: 3,900
Self-belief: 5/10
And the secret of golf is . . . new clubs, hopefully.

3 June, Day 247: 118 to go.
Sit-ups. Stretches. Crunches. Almost touch my left foot but then fall over.

I'm in a hotel room in Tallinn, Estonia. I stand in front of the mirror, in my boxers and socks. If the police burst in now they'll probably arrest me. The coat hanger in my hands would flummox them more than anything. They'd take some convincing that it represents a golf club – 'I did look for something else, officer, but there's barely enough space to swing a cat in here and I couldn't find a cat anyway and the only alternative was the lamp stand and that would have hit the ceiling'. They'd require even more convincing that my physical contortions bear any relation to golf (Pharro, Firkins and Malins are taking some convincing, too).

I wonder if they allow you the one phone call to a lawyer in Estonia? What should I say? 'I was working on my wrist roll, you see, while half-naked with a coat hanger, as one does . . . '

I reckon twenty years. Subject to good behaviour.

I've got six hours to kill before dinner. I'm in Tallinn to interview a businesswoman for a magazine. Julian, the photographer, is next door. We've spent the morning together and that's proved enough for both of us. Julian's into Formula One rather than coat hangers. He's probably stripping down an imaginary gearbox at the moment, or pretending to change Lewis Hamilton's tyres. God knows what Estonia's rapid-response police unit would make of that.

It's good to have some work at last. It's good to get out of the house. It's even good to converse with Julian rather than Emma, even if my shock-absorber small talk extends only so far. I feel useful. I'm contributing.

I've also got another job next week, in Gothenburg. Interviewing high-flying business executives may not be everyone's idea of glamour but they're more interesting than footballers. It's curtailing the golf, of course. No matter. I'm still waiting for my new clubs. I'll make do with coat hangers for now. And brain power.

Brain power's my latest theory. I'm going to think myself to better golf. I played some wretched stuff last month, but I'll spend the afternoon in front of my laptop and lower my handicap relying solely on the power of thought. Brilliant.

Malins deserves credit here. Bright chap, Malins. He has an inquiring mind. He believes in golf psychology and hypnosis. And during our last chipping lesson, I distinctly heard another penny drop.

There I was, happily practising, and Malins says: 'No, no, no!'

I was complaining at the time that my real problem was taking up the game in my forties, and playing for years without lessons. It was easy for him, beginning as a teenager. His first handicap was 22. He had lessons, avoided bad habits and was down to single figures in three months. Anybody could do that, I say haughtily.

Malins, a top-class hurdler and useful basketball player in his youth, is surprised average handicaps are so high. There are teachers who've forgotten how to stop talking, he says, and students who don't listen.

But for him the key lies in the art of practice.

So he watches me and says: 'No, no, no!'

I'm chipping with five balls, to a hole 20 feet away. The first rolls 10 feet past, the next 7 feet, then I get two to 5 and 4 feet and I'm pretty chuffed. Malins isn't.

'Practise with one ball,' he tells me in exasperation. 'How often do you get five chances during a match? Your play mimics your practice. So practise as you mean to play. One ball.'

Bloody obvious, of course. But then everything is. Afterwards.

'People aren't told how to practise,' Malins continues as I skull my next ball into the bushes. 'They expect to master new moves in one go. People hit balls on the range and call it practice. It's not. That's passing the time. It's a quick way to get worse. It's worse than doing nothing.

'Watch the pros. They're completely focused when they practise. The average guy? He's completely confused. There's so much information, so many tips, so many theories. Some of our members come in with a "move of the week". Every week.

'There's no secret. If there were, people would keep it just that – secret. But the idea that there might be one keeps people enticed. If you ever hear me talk about a secret you can shoot me.'

It's a nice thought. I'll bear it in mind.

But now I'm just outside the Estonian capital, in my boxers, Googling 'golf + secret of + best way to learn + revolutionary machine'.

I can't help the 'revolutionary machine' bit. I take Malins' point, of course, but surely he's missing a trick? Practising correctly and going through drills assiduously is all very well, but I still hanker after something altogether more ingenious.

I used to skydive. I know, it sounds glamorous and out of character. But it's true – Mr Blobby used to throw himself out of planes. You learnt by waiting for days for a break in the cloud, then tumbling out at 14,000 feet and spending a minute trying to stop doing somersaults. It took ages to improve – like golf, it's not exactly natural – until some bright spark invented a vertical wind tunnel, with air blasting up from the floor. Suddenly people could practise skydiving to their heart's content.

I'm hoping to unearth some such golfing machine. Something to automatically transform me into Ernie Els.

Without the wait. At the moment, the golf swing seems like a Rubik's Cube. You take it with you to the pub. You're getting somewhere and then it's your round. Whilst you're at the bar, your mates try to help. You return to find your cube in a worse mess than ever. That's golf for you. Take your eye off your swing for a second and it reverts into the Gordian knot.

I want golf to be like driving cars. You get in, your mind is a million miles away and suddenly, hey presto, you arrive at your destination without recalling a single detail of the journey. I want to be able to play like that. On auto-pilot. Without being breathalysed.

One hour later and I give up. There's no magic machine. There are hundreds of training aids on offer but no machine. More importantly, there's no consensus. Not a sniff of one.

I change tack. There simply must be a scientific way to learn a motor skill, turning theory into practice. What I need is a man in a white coat – a laboratory scientist, not a mental asylum doctor – who plays. I type again: 'The science of learning + golf + white coat + no mental asylums'.

I discover it takes 4,000 correct repetitions to change an ingrained motor skill. 4,000? What if you manage 3,999 and then botch the last one? Do you start all over again?

I wander off piste. I read about Fitts and Posner's 1967 cognitive learning theory. They postulate that learning begins with an instructional, cognitive phase, developing into an associative, then an autonomous phase when you act without thinking. It sounds wonderful. But I'm no nearer knowing how to get there.

I read about Schmidt's schema theory, about Vosniadou and Brewer's research, Adam's closed loop theory and the Fourier Analysis. The brain, I discover, is like a complex switchboard, with 45 miles of nerves monitoring impulses at 200mph. What we observe is mathematically translated into waveforms or neuromuscular commands which, in turn, make our muscle fibres twitch. That's how we move our limbs.

But what if you're rubbish at maths? What if your neuro transmitters and receptors aren't into golf? What if they send signals to the wrong muscles? Or to the right muscles in the wrong order? What if my receptors are dyslexic?

I keep searching. I find, contrary to what the golf magazines maintain, that there's no such thing as muscle memory (mine have amnesia, anyway). I delve into dyspraxia (difficulty with planning a sequence of co-ordinated movements – or, in layman's terms, me putting from 4 feet), kinesiology (how our body systems facilitate movement) and bio-mechanics.

It's getting late but I plough on. I'm on a roll. I make my most bizarre discovery on a German website. It's a research paper, written by an Australian bio-mechanics professor called Ross Sanders who's based in Scotland. You couldn't make it up. His thesis? That expertise in other sports can actually hinder, rather than help, your golf. It's too intriguing to ignore. I fire off a hopeful email in Sanders' general direction, asking for elucidation.

I find websites dedicated to teaching methods. They say there's too much 'how to' teaching. Too many teachers think they're the point, rather than their pupils. Telling isn't teaching and listening isn't learning. The art is to assist discovery, not dictate it.

Danish philosopher Soren Kierkegaard says you can't teach without first understanding your pupil. Others say some things are beyond instruction. Pablo Picasso says: 'You cannot teach painting, you must find it.' He does not say where golf swings are to be found.

There are studies on the efficacy of verbal, visual and kinaesthetic communication. Half of what we hear, apparently, is forgotten immediately, with the rest prone to misinterpretation.

Some people forget as much as they learn. It's a form of regression. In extreme cases, presumably, you end up knowing less than nothing. There's information on the difficulty of 'unlearning' an existing, error-ridden motor skill. And suddenly I'm back with Malins, as I stumble across 'deliberate practice'.

Ivan Galamian – an influential violin teacher, I read (my musical expertise extends to lugging Emma's keyboard to school every Thursday. God knows why she couldn't take up the recorder) – argued that great artists are defined by the quality, not quantity, of their practice.

People have always liked to take comfort in the belief that genius is God-given or in some way genetic – ie: 'It's not my fault that I'm such a clutz' – but Galamian felt that properly focused work, preferably beginning at a young age and monitored by a skilled teacher, was the key building block.

Musicians, apparently, must put in 10,000 hours of scales and arpeggios, equating to around ten years of practice, before they start winning international competitions. But, again, it's the how, not the how much. When most people practice, they do the things they have already mastered, rather than concentrating on what they can't do well in order to extend the range of their skills.

Take Mozart, that well-known child prodigy who popped out of the womb with a quill in one hand and the first of his symphonies in the other. But did he? Actually, Amadeus worked his socks off, right from his fourth birthday, when he began learning music under the gaze of his father, himself a skilled composer and famous teacher.

'Slammin' Sammy' Snead, winner of seven majors, is something of a golfing equivalent. He, too, was regarded as someone blessed with a magical gene, but as he told *Golf Digest*: 'People always said I had a natural swing. They thought I wasn't a hard worker. But when I was young, I'd play and practise all day, then practise more at night by my car's headlights. My hands bled. Nobody worked harder at golf than I did.'

I have a horrible, horrible thought. All my practice is wrong, lazy (my hands never look like bleeding) and unfocused, just as Malins was trying to tell me. Only it's even worse than he suspects.

Most of my golf has been honed in my lounge, when Emma and Jan are asleep. The key to the surreptitious practice of late-night, indoor irons is not to hit divots. That makes a noise. And ruins carpets. So I make sure I miss the carpet. Without realising, I raise my spine angle an inch or two going into impact. In effect, I'm practising topping the ball.

Then there's the putting. I aim at the carpet divider between lounge and kitchen. The kitchen has laminate flooring. Golf balls rumble on laminate. Jan does not appreciate midnight rumbling. So I ensure I putt short of the carpet edge. Ergo, I practise putting short.

Heck. I've just gone and wasted the first nine months of the best year of my life . . .

There's no hope. Golf's impenetrable, learning's impossible, my practice flawed and I'm His Grand Eminence, The King Of All Dorks. I've had enough. My head's exploding.

I decide to go next door and talk carburettors. It'll be a relief. One final Internet search unearths The World Scientific Congress of Golf. It's a quorum of boffins, writing incomprehensibly obscure tomes on all things golf. I send off some more emails, soliciting help.

I join Julian and discuss power boost valves, up-rated injectors, throttle bodies and fuel pumps. Later he shows me his Kimi Raikkonen toothbrush.

113 days to go: Gothenburg. Another business interview, another hotel room. The coat hangers are larger this time and easier to grip. You get two phone calls to a solicitor in Sweden. Julian reveals in an unguarded moment that he owns Ferrari pyjamas.

I get a text from Pharro.

'Hey T! H Grant in this pm 4 lesson with dave can u makit? chance 2 intrviu im!'

Bugger. Text back.

'Can't. Am in Gothenburg.'

He texts back.

'Isn't that where Batman lives?'

Oh dear . . .

110 days to go: Paxhill Park is no more. I'm now a Lindfield Golf Club member. The sale is complete and a revolution under way. They're smartening up the course and improving the greens. There are young, lithe, minuscule-handicap golfers everywhere, members of the Golf College. They all look like Justin Rose and hit the ball 320 yards. They're getting instruction from all manner of experts, including Denis Pugh, Colin Montgomerie's coach. While the Vets sulk in the bar, I sit down on a mound and take notes. Maybe I'll learn something.

I do learn something. I learn that sixteen-year-olds are made of elastic and that I cannot see a green 320 yards away, let alone a ball.

108 days to go: I haven't played for weeks. I'm not sure I want to. How can you swing a club with your head full of Schmidt, Vosniadou and Fourier? I opt for a cup of tea with neighbouring Juliet. She's a teacher. She listens to my woes.

'You need to relax,' she says. 'Why don't you drink a few beers before a round?'

Wow. What a left-field idea. The secret of golf – alcohol! Utterly brilliant. I'm inspired from my lethargy and load my clubs into a taxi. Just how many is a few beers, though? I order three pints. Marat smiles but says nothing. I set off, feeling wonderfully relaxed. I stop after nine holes for a top-up. I finish on 15 over – or was it 51?

I'm not convinced. Alcohol just makes you giggle. And visit the bushes more often than normal.

103 days to go: I receive two emails, the first unwelcome and the second quite the reverse.

First, Martin.

'Hi, bro, long time no speak.' There's a preamble, then 'by the way, I've broken 80 for the first time – shot 78 yesterday'.

Damn and blast! I'll never beat the bastard.

The second's from Ross Sanders – the Australian professor with Teutonic tendencies stranded in Scotland.

Sanders, it turns out, is at Edinburgh University. He's my man in the white coat! His research paper, in its original

English, is entitled: 'A Sporting Background: A Help or Hindrance when Learning the Golf Swing?'

Fantastic! Or perhaps not . . .

Sanders argues that his sporting past has been a disadvantage. He's had to 'unlearn' movements pertaining to other sports, in particular cricket, and hockey, and squash. Damn. I've played a bit of cricket, hockey and squash myself.

I suggest a round of golf. Sanders, extraordinarily, agrees. Edinburgh? Why, that's only 40 miles away from Dunblane, Neil McLellan's old course . . .

96 days to go: 9 a.m. I'm standing outside a mist-enveloped Edinburgh airport, expecting to be greeted by Professor Branestawm. Sanders will be short and almost bald and he'll blink behind milk-bottle glasses. He'll sport a white lab coat held together by string, with holes in his pockets patched up by brown packing tape. He'll peer down at his shoes while speaking ridiculously quickly, he'll lisp, and I won't understand a word.

Sanders duly marches up and introduces himself.

'Hi. Tony? Ross.'

He's tall and well built. Hair. No specs. No white coat. He speaks layman's sense from the outset. He does not look or sound like a professor. I feel cheated.

We drive to Dunblane and the sun breaks unexpectedly through.

'One of the three best days of the year so far,' chuckles Sanders. 'You've got lucky.'

But it's not luck. It's McLellan. He's looking down on us from the centre of a Heavenly Fairway. He's had words with the Golfing Deities. He's listening in, in the hope of learning something before the next Elysium monthly medal.

Over coffee, we agree to play first, chat later but I can't stop myself. Why, I ask, have average handicaps not come down? And any offers on the secret of golf?

Sanders talks about people failing to practise correctly and of ingraining bad habits over long periods. He refers to golf's small margins for error. He understands the golf swing, he adds, but plays only rarely. I should not expect a master class.

'I came to Scotland nine years ago, when I was offered the Sports Science Chair at Edinburgh University. I had a go as a teenager but never had lessons. I played lots of sport, including cricket and Aussie Rules, rugby union, basketball, squash and field hockey, intermingled with the usual Aussie pastimes like surfing. But I came here looking for something more sedate and Scotland is, after all, the home of golf.

'My thesis was in sports bio-mechanics and I studied motor control as well. Golf's fascinating from both perspectives. I've published a few papers on it. I probably know more about what to do – and what can go wrong – than most but I haven't had the opportunity to put the science into practice. I can also get too involved in the theory. Sometimes I do better when I stop thinking and just smash it.'

We head for the 1st tee and I proceed to play the best round of my life. I play way, way, way beyond myself.

Dunblane is much more challenging than Lindfield but I'm inspired from the moment I flush a three-wood down the middle of the 1st. All the luck goes my way, too. I bounce over bunkers, I find great lies, I hole a 40-foot downhill, left-to-righter. I get the impression McLellan is drifting invisibly ahead of us, kicking my ball back on to the fairway.

I am 2 over after nine and 1 over after eleven. But then I lose my head on the 13th, attempting a ridiculously over-ambitious escape from the second-degree rough. The ball goes nowhere. Twice. I treble-bogey.

Sanders, meanwhile, is having no luck at all. His best shots are sensational, but always at exactly the wrong moment. He hits four or five imperious three and five-wood approaches which fly the green and disappear into knee-high heather. As for his putting, it isn't so much rusty as blighted with metal fatigue.

The par-five 18th sums up the day. I slice my second short and right, while Sanders magically threads his three-wood through the trees and makes the green in two. He three putts for par. I pitch over a bunker to 2 feet and birdie.

I finish with a mind-boggling 7 over. My second round in singles – and away from Lindfield! There's no anticlimax this time. I've played as well as I can. I've become a golfer within a year! I feel like screaming.

We retire to the bar and toast McLellan's memory. Then, for an hour and a half, Sanders blows my mind.

He encapsulates his thinking in one simple, auto-biographical story. As a young cricketer, he opened his team's batting and bowling. One winter, he devoted himself to non-stop bowling practice in his back yard.

Result? The next season his bowling was so wretched that he had to give it up.

'It turned out that our back yard was two yards short. In effect, I was practising bowling the wrong length.

'In motor control terms, you develop what's called an attractor state in your co-ordination. As a bowler, you release the ball at a certain point. That winter, I changed this attractor state so that I was releasing it later. Once I got on to a full-sized pitch I couldn't revert. All I could do was bowl bouncers.

'When I had my first golf lessons, I didn't realise that I had attractors from other sports. Basically, I found that my cricket, squash and hockey movement patterns didn't work for golf. You could say golf has never forgiven me for playing other sports first.'

I feel the same way. I tell Sanders I've tried repeating Pharro's foreign-feeling moves on a daily basis but with only partial success.

Sanders then delivers a bombshell. I am, it turns out, thirty years out of date.

'What you're trying to do – that is, reduce the golf swing to a repeatable, unchanging computer programme for your body to follow and which gets your limbs in exactly the right place at the right time – was in vogue in the 70s and 80s. Modern thinking has changed. Variability of practice is being encouraged now.'

I look witless.

'Look,' he explains, 'you go to a driving range and hit off a flat mat in a dry, sheltered bay. You get reasonably consistent. But what happens when you get out on the course? The lie's never flat, there's divots, there's rough, there's gusting wind and rain.

'People market machines to get you swinging in a perfect, identical plane. For me, they're a gimmick. They've never been proven to work and, arguably, can do more harm than good.

'I know that everyone goes on about consistency and how you should practise the same things over and over. That definitely does have benefits. But it has to be intermingled with reality – with varied practice.

'Trying to repeat an identical swing takes away your variety and your body's natural tendency to explore the movement possibilities. Anybody seeking a perfect swing is probably wasting his time. That's not how it's done. Basically, the body's too complex for that to work. Each of your limbs can move with six degrees of freedom, can move in three directions of trans-lation and three directions of rotation. It's too much to ask of your nervous system to completely control such freedom.'

Oh great. So I'll never possess Ernie's swing? I've just shot the best round of my life and I'm doing everything wrong?

Well, yes.

'Recent analysis shows that top players don't confine their swing to one plane,' Sanders adds. 'It varies as it goes back and down. They move their heads more than the rest of us. We're so obsessed with the "Don't Move Your Head" tip that we become constrained by it.

'The real difference is that the best players get it right where it matters − at impact. The rest of their swing may change according to circumstance but at impact they adjust and invariably get the angle of the club and its direction of travel just right.

Sanders sees I'm struggling, so he resorts to imagery.

'Imagine a long jumper. He runs up and tries to hit the take-off board spot on. He measures out his stride pattern. But then the wind starts blowing. So he compensates and still gets his body in the right position at take-off.'

Sanders tells me to imagine every possible combination of physical movements within the golf swing as a series of spots on a flat surface.

'Now you roll a marble on to that surface and hope it lands on the right spot − the combination where your limbs work correctly to perform a good swing. Sometimes the marble rolls off in another direction – you duff the shot, basically. But sometimes it rolls very close to where you want it to go.

'To give the marble a better chance of reaching the right spot, you hollow out the area around it, dig a bit of dirt out, say, to attract the marble. The more you practise, the more you hollow out. And the more likely it is that the marble – as long as it lands in the general area – will spiral down to the right spot.

'In golfing terms, that means your backswing can be variable but you're still right at impact.'

But what happens if The Man In The Street digs a hollow in the wrong place? Surely he'll be attracted towards a bad swing? Isn't that what people are doing at golf ranges?

'That's right. Then we have to find a way of weakening that attractor, by filling in that hollow and digging another in the correct place. The frustration is that we may gradually begin swinging better – rolling our marble to the right co-ordinate, if you like – but that now and then we'll revert to the entrenched "bad habit". Everybody does. That's where coaching and video feedback can help to identify the right hollow.

'Sometimes, we also mess up by trying to hit too hard. That's like rolling the marble too fast. It bounces out of the hollow rather than spiralling into it. It's no good putting too much energy into the system.'

Sanders points out that there's a gulf between scientists, teachers and pupils.

'You can't expect practitioners to study scientific journals and understand what scientists are saying. I feel lots of what we do is wasted – it doesn't filter down to grass roots or get applied. We need a go-between – a translator.'

As for golf teachers, they know how to play but 'basically

regurgitate what they've been told. In most cases they probably don't understand the scientific principles. They manipulate your body but don't give you a mechanical reason for it.

'Some, subconsciously, try to impose a model on their students. But it's pointless trying to swing like Tiger or Ernie. They're different. They have different limb lengths, strengths and flexibilities.'

Suddenly the sun vanishes. McLellan, clearly, has heard enough, even if I haven't. The Edinburgh mist rolls into Dunblane. The temperature drops from 22 degrees to 14 within 5 miles as we drive back.

We talk more. About pre-shot routines, and body segments and how the crack of a whip is actually a mini sonic boom. How golf is not natural. How Sanders' wife Fiona, a university senior lecturer, swings a golf club while humming 'The Blue Danube'. How Sanders carried out putting tests on Jack Nicklaus at the 2000 Open.

At the airport we shake hands.

'You've done really well there, mate,' says Sanders. 'You've got some good attractors in place.'

'It was nice to meet you, Ross. And beat you,' I reply. 'If I can beat a boffin, perhaps I can beat my brothers.'

He laughs.

'There's no substitute for practice. Just make it varied.'

I treat myself to a coffee. Seven over – away from Lindfield – and with a witness! I practise my body turn in front of the airport lounge windows. A toddler comes over and copies me, only better, before his mother drags him away.

I wonder if they really do have golf courses in heaven.

93 days to go: Roy's returning to work. He's not taken to house husbandry. He expresses himself through business success. He never looked completely comfortable holding his daughter's pink bag on the school run. I'll miss him. He'll stop talking to chocolate biscuits, get fit, lose weight and regain his sense of purpose. And then there'll be only one hippo. Me. Bit depressing, really.

Talking of depression, Jan comes home with a newspaper article. Apparently it's OK to feel down. According to an international study, middle age is universally miserable. That's when people realise they're not living up to their aspirations. I've known that since kindergarten.

The good news, though, is that we cheer up later; seventy-year-olds are as upbeat as twenty-year-olds. Presumably because they've got Alzheimer's and haven't got a clue what's going on. So happiness is U-shaped. Like a good bunker shot. On average, global grumpiness bottoms out at the age of forty-eight and a half. I should be altogether more gregarious this time next year.

92 days to go: I'm £350 poorer, after seeing a doctor about my lack of serious daily exercise, suspect eating habits and my ME. Jan and I agreed to have comprehensive health checks when we reached forty. She kept her word and passed with flying colours. I dreamt up a threadbare excuse and stuck to it for eight years.

The doctor takes my blood pressure, checks my cholesterol and makes me blow into tubes. He makes me drop my trousers. When my back is turned — God, I'm naïve — he surprises me with a rubber glove.

My results are not as bad as I feared. But some mild exercise every now and then – golf does not count, for some reason – and a balanced diet would be a good idea.

'Are you depressed?' the doctor asks suddenly.

Depressed? Of course not. I'm just a tad lethargic and lacking in motivation, that's all.

The doctor's not convinced.

'Your ME may be the root cause of your tiredness but anti-depressants could help. I've known it work with other patients. Why not chat to your GP?'

The man's clearly an idiot. And I'm still not too happy about that rubber-glove trick of his. I certainly don't need drugs. I just need a few more pars and birdies.

FIFTEEN

CLAUSE 23 AND A CAT CALLED EDWARD

'"After all, golf is only a game," said Millicent. Women say these things without thinking. It does not mean that there is a kink in their character. They simply don't realise what they are saying'

— *P.G. Wodehouse*

Weight: OK, I admit it – it's crept up.
Waist measurement: I admit it – larger.
Diet: Eating Emma's left-overs is the perennial problem. And Jan's.
Alcohol: If Jan would only cut back, I could cut back.
Chronic Fatigue: Bad news – back to 2–3 hours sleep a day.
Official handicap: 21.8
Rounds: 21
Average score: 17.42 over
Average score over last ten rounds: 15.2 over
Average score over last five rounds: 14 over
Eagles: 0
Longest drive: 277 yards (6 May, Lindfield, 18th)
Range balls: 4,100
Self belief: 8/10
And the secret of golf is . . . varied practice and 'The Blue Danube'.

1 July, Day 275: 90 to go.

I'm in love. I sit in the kitchen and stare adoringly. My new golf clubs stare back (they may not be quite as pleased. They'd probably hoped for Sergio). Occasionally, I stroke one of them.

I've just collected them from Precision Golf. I take Emma. She doesn't want to come and wears her grumpy face for the entire journey. She is very, very adept at grumpy faces. Riled, I counter-attack. I tell her it's about time she started helping more around the house.

Grumpy silence.

'And you must start cleaning your bedroom on your own.'

Silence.

'There were clothes everywhere this morning.'

Silence.

'I think you've got too many clothes, to be honest . . .'

'I just haven't got enough hangers,' comes the truculent reply.

At Precision, Emma sniffs out a bowl of sweets next to the magazines and clears it out while I'm talking to Cooper and Davey.

'That was fun, can we go back tomorrow?' she asks on the way back.

I'm loath to use the clubs. I don't want to spoil them. Or am I just frightened that they won't work? Or, more pertinently, that I won't? I'm not stupid. I know they're excellent clubs. I understand the issue here.

87 days to go: Sit-ups. Stretches. Touch ankles.

I risk it, drive to Lindfield and run into, of all people, James.

'What are you doing here?' I ask.

'I've returned from the dead.'

There's been a rethink. James, once surplus to requirements, is now regarded as an asset. He'll help out, while operating his business from a new office which he'll build himself.

He looks at my new clubs with interest.

I tell him about my round with Professor Branestawm.

'Seven over? And no witnesses again?' says James. 'Or rather, one – an Australian professor at a Scottish university who publishes in German?'

And he pulls a lopsided, irony-laden smile.

'Anyway,' he adds, 'it doesn't count. You said you were only counting your Lindfield and Poult Wood rounds.'

I go to the range. There's no cataclysmic, jaw-dropping improvement. But the new irons feel different and the ball flies well, perhaps with a little less effort. And I love my new rescue club. And the three-wood goes straighter.

The only trouble's the driver. I can't get the ball off the deck.

Bernard Firkins spots me chipping.

'Still using the Vivien Saunders putt-chip, I see?' he says.

Saunders? Saunders? Of course, I'd forgotten! Didn't we discuss her, months ago? Didn't she invent women's golf or something?

I return home to my statistics. They don't take long. James is right, of course. Dunblane doesn't count. Which means I played just once last month, and even then I was half-cut. I'm averaging 14 over for my last five rounds, with three months left. I must pack in some more rounds.

I text James after some cursory Dysoning: 'Game?'

I get Emma's felt tips out and she helps me create a golf chart identifying my strengths and weaknesses. We agree to call it homework. I reckon my long game's three shots better than it was, my short game's worth four, and the same for my putting. The physio must be worth one. So there's twelve shots. So I should be playing off 12. If my clubs offer me a further five, why . . .

Emma's got bored with the chart. She draws a tin of baked beans.

'That's really good,' I say, adding baked beans to my shopping list.

'It's not as good as Andy Warhol's,' she replies.

It turns out her class have done a lesson on Warhol. Blimey. So she does listen occasionally.

I Google 'Vivien+Saunders', expecting an obituary. It turns out she's very much alive. Turns out she was a professional player and celebrated teacher who won the women's British Open in 1977. She has her own website. She also has attitude.

Apparently she regained her amateur status after a protracted fight with the Royal & Ancient. So she no longer gives lessons, unless it's for charity. There are some photographs, though, of her cat, Edward. Edward, apparently, is happy to offer tuition.

So I email Edward and ask him 1) for a lesson 2) could he set up an interview with Vivien?

86 days to go: I visit Doc. My ME's back. I'm sleeping between two and three hours a day again. What have I been up to recently, she asks? Anything out of the ordinary? Well, I did fly to Dunblane and back in a day to play eighteen holes of golf . . .

'No great surprise then, is it?' she says, wearily.

I leave with a prescription for anti-depressants. Apparently they won't turn me into a junkie. There'll be no tell-tale signs. Nothing to be ashamed of. And the pills won't work for a month, so don't give up on them. And no more Dunblanes-and-back.

Doc also gives me a letter for the local gym. I am to be assessed before undertaking a light exercise programme.

'This is important,' she says. 'It should help, along with the pills.'

I nod gravely. I collect the anti-depressants but the gym appointment letter slips my mind and goes into the washing machine along with my jeans.

I do, though, decide to contact a nutritionist. That should be less tiring. And it could be worth one extra shot off my handicap. And, according to playground mum Sarah, I should contact her Pilates teacher. Good for body control, apparently. Another shot? At this rate I'll be scratch in no time.

85 days to go: Emma: 'If God dies, do we die?'

Christ knows. Actually that's quite a neat answer. I avoid the temptation, though, and resort to the tried and trusted.

'Ask your mum.'

We go to Knightsbridge. I want to see Hugh Grant. Emma wants to see 'Andeee'. She's delighted. I'm disappointed. Grant's on a film shoot or receiving an award or brawling with photographers somewhere. I make do with a lesson. My wrists are passable, but, as usual, I'm all arm lift rather than shoulder turn. I'm 'disconnected'. I'm in a rut again. A passing mention of my Dunblane success cuts no ice.

On the way back, Emma says hello to the doorman outside Harvey Nichols. She particularly admires his top hat and long coat. His name, we discover, is Tim and, extraordinarily, he's a friend of one of our neighbours. How weird is that. 'It's a small world,' I tell Emma. Now she wants to go back to London, to see

'Andeee and the man with the big hat who lives in a small world'.

84 days to go: My brother Roger presents me with a motorised golf trolley. I'm lost for words, which is rare. Goodness knows what it costs. He thinks it might be worth a shot or two to me. I'll be playing to plus 2 in a matter of weeks! Plus 4 and I can turn professional.

83 days to go: I spend an hour on the range before playing James. I still can't get the new driver high enough, although it's going straight. James likes the look of the irons – 'I might have given you slightly lighter shafts, though' – and the woods but he thinks the driver needs more loft.

We discuss handicaps. James is stuck on 12. I'm stuck on 21.8 but complain that this month's medal was washed out and I couldn't make the last one. I reckon I'm nearer 13 or 14 but what can you do?

'Why don't you hand in three cards and ask the handicap committee to consider them under Rule 19.4?' says James.

Apparently handicaps can be adjusted in special circumstances. But there's a catch. Don't forget that for official purposes, says James, we play off the whites.

But I'm full of bravado. I won that medal off the white tees, after all. What's a few extra yards here and there?

'Watch this!' I trumpet. I march to the back of the 1st tee, hook my drive, shank my second and open with a triple bogey.

But I par the next five, my slightly ill-timed long game salvaged by my chipping, and I'm 5 over at the turn. I begin with a spate of bogeys on the way back and – I realise only later – I'm 9 over with four to play.

On the par-five 15th, however, I produce the perfect hole;

as good a drive as I can play to 265 yards, a better four-wood than I can ever hope to play to just short of the green, a bump-and-run nine-iron to 5 feet – I can't bump-and-run to save my life – and a putt for birdie.

I follow that with par, par, bogey.

Nine over. I've done it – with the best witness I could hope for! I've all but completed the challenge, almost three months early! Two rounds in single figures! (three including Dunblane). One of them off the white tees! I . . . am . . . a . . . golfer!

This time, though, I feel relief rather than exultation. If anything, it was classic curate's egg. I chipped well and putted nicely. As for the rest, well, I don't want to go on like a scratched CD but, strangely, I still don't feel as good as I thought I would.

More than anything, I'm glad the project's pretty much over. Except that it isn't. James takes my card.

'I'll hand it in for you. We've still got to get you that new handicap, so you need two more – signed by a reliable witness. Not by some fictitious professor. Play like that again and you could end up with a better handicap than me.'

A better handicap than James? The guy who's taught me half of what I know? That would be something. It's a nice thought. But it's all about beating my three brothers now. I've got to learn how to score well regularly for that to happen.

79 days to go: A book arrives from Amazon – *The Secret of Golf.* I know, I know – I'm not meant to be reading tips or looking for miracles but surely I deserve a little celebration. And, after months of self-imposed golf magazine/Golf Channel abstinence, I couldn't resist the title.

Actually, it's the title on the back that really grabs me. '47

Holy Grails', it reads. Which just about sums it up. There's no one secret. There's 47. Or 75. Make that 96. Or how about 1,258? There are as many secrets, I fancy, as there are golfers. Perhaps the important thing is simply not to try them all at once. Wasn't it Harvey Penick who likened golf tips to aspirin? One may relieve your headache temporarily. But down the whole bottle and you'll need your stomach pumped.

76 days to go: 9 a.m. My first appointment with the nutritionist. I like her a lot. She speaks sense.

It's all about balance. And avoiding crisps and chocolate. I must not eat Emma's left-overs. Snacking is a no-no. Porridge is good. So's houmous on a rice cake. And nuts.

I decide not to go again. I know all this already. I just can't apply it. I don't need a nutritionist. I need someone to guard the fridge with a 12-bore.

2 p.m. My first appointment with the Pilates instructor. I like her a lot. She speaks sense.

It's all about proper breathing and pelvic floor exercises. I'm surrounded by women in Lycra leotards drinking purified water. I'm in a pair of Stanley Matthews shorts, ill-fitting trainers and a frayed 'Meatloaf European Tour 1999' T-shirt.

I feel out of place. It's a self-image thing. I decide not to go again.

73 days to go: James and I meet up for my second qualifying round just as the monsoon breaks. We spend two hours in the bar, watching the course submerge. We're about to call the coastguard when the rain stops. What the heck. Let's give it a whirl. It'll be a bit moist, that's all. James has to get away by midday, though, so we decide on speed golf – it will be a

practice round, with no warm-up, practice swings or lining up putts.

'You're not exactly a fast player anyway,' says James. 'A quicker tempo might just help.'

I sprint around in 23 over, my worst score since my year began. I fail to hit my new driver above ankle height. But I learn a hugely useful lesson.

My play, believe it or not, is not as bad as the score suggests, considering the glutinous conditions. I just get myself into a couple of serious scrapes.

First I pull a low drive and it rolls into some tree roots. The shot's not disastrous but the consequences are. Two air shots later and I declare the ball unplayable. I take an eight.

Then I tug a seven-iron on to a sodden greenside bank. Again, the shot's not disastrous, it's what follows. I can just see the ball. My attempted chip bobbles one yard down the bank. I can no longer see it. Without drawing breath, I chop again. Same result. I now have no idea where it is. My third shot fails to make contact. I take a drop. I take a ten.

I feel bruised. Old Tom waxes eloquently on the subject.

I also manage an OB but my round is defined by those two shots, the drive and the seven-iron. Bad luck was involved – if I'd landed a couple of yards either side . . . – but my judgement let me down. Not for the first time, I overestimated my ability.

I've been here before. Your score depends largely on your bad – or unfortunate – shots. A healthy dose of realism never goes amiss. And stupidity just compounds things.

Thank goodness we declared it practice. I tear up my card and go home to a hot bath and a phone message. It's from Vivien Saunders. She invites me to tea.

I phone Precision Golf and, feeling like the archetypal bad

workman, demand more loft to my driver. I try to sound indignant, but I know what Davey and Cooper must be thinking. I'm thinking it myself. It's me, not the club.

71 days to go: 10.30 a.m. I wouldn't describe Delia Smith — sorry, Vivien Saunders — as formidable. That would be to understate the case. Which is odd, for someone with impossibly small feet, a Women's Institute politeness and a close resemblance to a TV cook (I'm tempted, indeed, upon meeting her, to complain about her broccoli soufflé but I let it pass).

We meet at Abbotsley in Cambridgeshire, one of her two golf courses. She orders tea and scones and biscuits and apologises for Edward's absence. He's out rabbitting. Saunders — Open champion, one of the founders of the women's European Tour, the winner of tournaments world-wide, a qualified lawyer, successful businesswoman and published author — will have to suffice.

We sit down in armchairs, in a quiet corner. She's as I expected, only a bit more wind-blown. She's short and cuddly, enveloped in a thick jumper and corduroy trousers. She reminds me of favourite aunts and early Sunday evenings in front of crackling open fires. She speaks in a soft, gentle voice while pouring our first cups.

I tell her I love the myth-busting simplicity of her short-game video. I tell her about my golfing challenge. Then I ask her about average handicaps and Saunders is out of the traps like a greyhound on amphetamines. She remains perfectly polite and in control, there's no arm-waving or ranting, but there's a steely edge to her now. And she talks twice as fast. My favourite aunt has been replaced by someone altogether more determined and resolute. Boudica, say, on her day off.

Someone used to getting her own way without having to resort to scythed war chariots. I sit back, cling on to my chair and pray my recorder holds out.

'Well, for a start, the whole structure of golf's ridiculous. It's just about the only sport played off a handicap system, unless you happen to be ridiculously short and like riding horses.

'We used to play much more scratch golf. My mother and her friends were low single-figure handicap players. If your husband played off, say, 20, well, that was too embarrassing to mention in public.'

I start to sink ever lower in my chair. . .

'Today, it's all Stableford and people think 20's quite good. Which it isn't. So where's the incentive to get better? You hear people say he or she must be good, he's won a bunch of cups and plaques. He or she shows them off at every opportunity. Well, he or she probably keeps winning the Granny Trophy or the Great Great Granddad Monthly Stableford, playing off 36 or 28. Big deal. I once co-wrote a book with Nick Faldo. He didn't have a cup or plaque in sight.

'We hold society competitions here. They're invariably "won" by high handicappers. Towards the bottom of the leaderboard you'll always find some poor bugger playing off 4 with 35 points who's shot 77 on a course he doesn't know. He or she is an excellent golfer but nobody cares.

'The winners come preening into the shop and you want to say: "You poor devil, you can't even break 90." But instead you manage to mumble: "That's not too bad." Actually, it's crap.'

And I sit there, blinking, and wondering if I've really just heard Delia Smith say 'bugger' and 'crap'. Pharro would love this. Smoke is pouring out of my recorder. Boudica is resorting to her war chariot after all. She's not strident.

She's not vehement. She's just unstoppable, that's all. I'm beginning to think I'd rather grapple with a grizzly.

'Handicaps? Actually,' Saunders says, 'I believe they've got worse.

'Just go to Sunningdale. There's a scorecard on the wall, showing Bobby Jones's round of 66 in an Open qualifier in 1926. It records the clubs he used. It's incredible. "Driver, brassie [two-wood]. Driver, spoon [three-wood)." He hit thirty-three hickory-shafted strokes and thirty-three putts – with a ball you wouldn't recognise as a golf ball today – and every hole was played in three or four. I think he hit a driver and two-wood into the 18th. Today, pros hit a two-iron and a nine.

'So it's easy to see why the elite score better now. But your average male still can't break 90. I can play off the men's tees with a putter and a seven-iron and do it. Which means, let's be blunt, that they can't play. Oh sure, with the new equipment, even Harry The Hacker can hit 290 yards. He can hit humongous distances. But that's not good golf.'

I'm offered more Darjeeling, but it's not a ceasefire, merely an opportunity to bury a few of the dead before a recommencement of hostilities.

'I mean, imagine playing rugby off handicap! You versus Jonny Wilkinson. We'll put a paper bag over his head to even things up. Or let's make Colin Jackson Fosbury-flop over 6-foot hurdles while we jump over diddy ones. It's laughable.

'Paula Radcliffe's from Bedford, just down the road. I'll challenge her to a handicap marathon. I'll have a 21-mile start – that should be enough – and I'll win, little old me, and jump up and down in delight and Radcliffe will bob in and I'll say "better luck next time" and I'll offer her a few training tips while everyone clamours for my autograph. And, of course, I'll get a cup or a plaque.

'It's like the Emperor's new clothes. It's a pretence. Somebody hopeless is slightly less hopeless on a given day, so they get a prize. It's farcical. But it happens every day at golf clubs.'

Another scone perhaps?

'When was the last time you got a sport's prize? When you were in short trousers and won the egg and spoon race and got a tube of Smarties, that's when. Golf's so childish. People marching about in ridiculous uniforms – it's like a prep school's dress code.

'The game's run as a pastime, not a sport. By whom? High handicappers, that's who. Go to Haywards Heath hockey or rugby club and you expect the captain to be a good player. Everyone wants to get into the first team and beat rival clubs. They train several times a week. In golf clubs, people don't train. They play each other. Good players are resented. Golf club captains tend to be retired old duffers. They live on committees and wear badges and blazers.

'Golf needs patrons with lots of money and no time. Instead, we've got people with no money and too much time. The lunatics are running the asylum.'

She smiles. But it doesn't mask the frustration. Saunders has spent her whole golfing life at war with officialdom.

Having represented England and Britain at junior level, she came runner-up in the British Amateur Championship as a nineteen-year-old while at university. It was then that she committed a horrendous crime. She enquired about the opportunities offered by professional golf.

'I was reported to the R&A and forced to turn pro, just for

making that enquiry. The R&A used to do that, back then. That forced my hand. So I started teaching and went out to play on the LPGA Tour in America.'

She became the first woman living outside the US to get a tour card but returned within a few years to care for her mother. She then directed her energies towards launching the women's European Tour, while winning trophies across the world.

When her attempts to become a club professional failed – 'I took the London Borough of Richmond to court for sexual discrimination on the back of that' – she gave up golf and became a partner in a firm of solicitors.

That did not stop her winning the Open, however, or acting as national coach to the English Ladies' Golf Association for almost two decades, with Laura Davies and Alison Nicholas among her pupils. Throughout, however, she was still deemed a professional.

She returned to the game by buying a course and setting up a golf school. Having missed so much golf, she took on the R&A's 'blazered buffoons' yet again to regain her amateur status. It took three years, even though she hadn't played on tour for around two decades.

'Archaic rules like these have ruined the lives of so many golfers,' she says. 'Look at all the young pros who end up serving behind tills in golf clubs – they're wonderful players but fail to make it to the very top and then find there's little meaningful competitive golf for them. The PGA – the Professional Golfers' Association . . . for me, that should stand for "Promotes Greater Apathy".'

Saunders' CV extends in all directions, including golf books and videos, a psychology degree, an MBA, membership of MENSA, British Sports Coach of the Year (twice) and an OBE.

Golf teaching, however, has always been close to her heart.

'To be honest, I was more interested in teaching than playing. I was always going to teach something,' she says. 'I was born to it. Teaching is people orientated. Playing's quite lonely. There's not many who do both.'

Deficient teaching, she says, is another cause of bad golf.

'To teach, you have to care passionately about helping people. People find golf incredibly difficult. When beginners look down, the ball looks the size of a pea. But most people aren't taught by academically qualified people. The PGA rejects the idea of specially trained teachers.

'Then there's the problem of pros not saying the same things. Some even like to sound complicated, to create a sense of mystique. In a nutshell, there's not enough coaching, it's badly taught and it's expensive.'

More Darjeeling, and another respite. My recorder has melted.

There's more, of course. Much more.

Saunders is at her best when ruffled.

Saunders on sexism: 'Go into most clubs and you see imposing, nauseating boards inscribed with the words "Club Captain" and "Ladies Captain". So there are two sexes in golf – ladies . . . and clubs.'

On golf's rulers: 'It's a marvellous game ruined by ridiculous people – a game of mis-hits run by misfits.'

On hierarchies: 'In most clubs, the pecking order runs from past presidents and captains to ordinary men members, juniors, dogs, ladies, artisans and greenkeepers. In some clubs, the ladies fall below juniors, dogs and artisans. Ladies occasionally get commended for something – like making sandwiches. Greenkeepers are beyond the pale. They never get thanked for anything.'

On the R&A: 'There is, apparently, no rule prohibiting women from becoming members. It's just that, out of 2,400-odd members, not one is a woman. There's also no rule which prohibits an R&A member from using an elephant or camel to carry his clubs. Elephants and camels, in fact, would probably be preferable to women.'

On arrogance: 'There's plenty of arrogance in golf but you rarely find a really good player who's arrogant. They know full well that they can hit horrendous shots or miss short putts. They accept it. Just don't rub their noses in it. I remember Mark James once topping a shot into the rough at the Open at Lytham. A journalist asked him how far it had gone. "I walked it but I didn't fucking count it," was the reply.'

I finish with my traditional request for golf's secret.

'You've cracked the worst part by getting down from 24,' she says. 'You've dealt with the glaring errors.

'One thing, though. There's a lot of emphasis on the back-swing nowadays. You see people peering back over their shoulder, as if to make sure the club's still there. But the backswing's just preparation. If you want to keep looking backwards, take up rowing. It's the through swing which matters.

'Golf's just another racket game. The real secret is to feel the face of the club. Most people's concept of the end of the g   club finishes at the end of the grip.

'But put a squash racket in someone's hand and they instinctively know how the head must react to hit the ball left or right.

'Imagine buttering a bread roll. You don't wonder where

your elbow goes. All you're aware of is the end of the knife. It feels like the end of your finger. That's what I teach.'

Saunders is decelerating. She's my aunt again. She gets up. She has a round booked and needs to change. I thank her for the royal entertainment.

I hang around, to watch her tee off. It's too cold for shorts, and too warm for a bobble hat. She re-emerges sporting both. She cracks the ball straight down the middle of the 1st fairway and marches after it. Edward appears from nowhere and pads along behind her, riding shotgun.

'He usually walks the first two holes, then picks her up on the way back, down the 13th,' says the receptionist.

I drive home, concentrating on buttering bread rolls and quite convinced that Saunders should be in charge. Not just of golf. Of everything. We'd still have an empire if she were.

68 days to go: I miss the Lindfield Golf Club championship, in favour of Emma's ballet show. She and her friends prance about the stage as the 101 Dalmatians – at least, I think that's what they're meant to be. In their parents' eyes, they're unutterably cute and a huge source of pride. To anybody else, I imagine, they'd be a bunch of small girls in ill-fitting black and white leotards with doubtful senses of rhythm and direction. They'd be right, of course. We applaud wildly, as if we're at the Bolshoi.

I hear later that Dan, Paxhill's greenkeeper, won the championship. Saunders would approve. The event has been known to descend into rancour, bitterness, bile and wild accusations in the past but passes off this time without fuss. Everyone at Lindfield is very disappointed.

67 days to go: I watch some women's golf on TV. The Koreans, Japanese and Chinese wipe the floor with the rest and I find myself wondering whether golf is, in fact, a martial art. You know the sort of thing – power through controlled restraint.

As a teenager, I adored a book entitled *Zen in the Art of Archery*. It was about a Westerner trying to learn Zen Buddhism in a monastery. He was taught to lose his sense of ego through archery and its series of simple, repetitive movements. Lose your self-awareness within mundane repetition and you'll hit the target. That's golf.

Perhaps I should become a Buddhist. Perhaps it would help my short game. But it probably involves a fair bit of study and I'm now in a hurry. I look up *Zen in the Art of Archery*. It's out of print.

66 days to go: An extraordinary thing happens this morning. I forget whether I part my hair on the right or left. I try both but still cannot decide. That can't be good.

Precision Golf come up trumps. My driver's back. It's still 10 degrees but the shaft has a lower kick-point. James thinks 11.5 degrees would be better but what does he know? Things are about to change for ever.

27 July/29 July, Day 300/302: 63 to go.

And so things change for ever.

My second and third handicap rounds at Lindfield with James represent the highlight of my year. I can't imagine matching them.

Under pressure to perform, I fire two consecutive, unprecedented rounds of 75 (5 over par). On the 18th green, James and I shake hands solemnly and in silence. There is nothing to be said. I have suddenly, somehow, scored the golf of my dreams.

James takes the cards to the handicap committee, along with my opening 9 over, while predicting a revised handicap of around 7 or 8. A single-figure handicap! I have massively exceeded expectations!

I could write a whole book on these two rounds alone. Except that I couldn't. In fact, I can barely remember a thing about either. Yes, I've scored the golf of my dreams, but I haven't played it.

I go through my cards. There's no escaping it. Neither round was that special. How did I do it? What is the secret of golf? Goodness knows . . . but whatever it is, it's not spectacular.

Round one is built around some great chipping, a handful of putts holed from around 8 feet and some very acceptable 'bad' shots. If anything, and insane as it sounds, it's the unexpectedly good shots that let me down. Two of my approaches are so once-in-a-lifetime-well-struck that they go long and into deep rough for bogeys. I adored those two shots. My scorecard calls them mistakes.

Meanwhile my new driver leaves me cold. I hit the ball straight but low and rarely beyond 240 yards. It works. But eye-popping it is not.

Round two is a collection of conservative, sensible mis-hits, some decent pitches, good chips and five great putts. I think it was Hogan who said he hit only about four perfect shots a round. Putts and chips aside, I don't hit any.

Incredible. Baffling and bemusing. I think back to Dan's 68 – is this how he felt? I score like a god but play like a sensible earthling. I barely hit a long shot demanding recall. It feels like Roquefort without the Sauternes. It feels like a good day at the office, not a great day away from it. It feels a bit like a job, however well done. It feels short of passion and drama. Old Tom is so bored he doesn't even bother to try to distract me.

In fact, the only memorable shot comes from James. He plays like a donkey. One of his rounds concludes miserably on 20 over par. Perhaps there are only so many successful golf swings available in the world on any given day, so he had to do without. But on the tough, uphill 7th, he hits an approach to die for. It's a five-iron, it makes a sound never to be forgotten and screams towards its target like tracer fire and I know then, immediately, that I've just witnessed a perfect golf shot.

But my game? Etched in the memory? Etched in sand, more like. Etched in water.

Is that really it? Is this what I wanted?

Look, I'm very proud. The numbers are phenomenal. But – call me a killjoy – I'm not quite sure how grand it really was. Good putts and chips still don't speak to me, not very loudly. There must be lots of ways to score 5 over. I'm not sure my way was the most thrilling, that's all.

I go home with a headache. I hate to admit to a sense of anticlimax, but it feels as if something's missing. I don't text anyone.

SIXTEEN

THE BIGGEST JOKE IN THE WORLD

'The golf swing is like a suitcase into which we are trying to pack one too many things'

— John Updike

Weight: 13st 10lb (same as the start of the year).
Waist measurement: See start of year.
Diet: See start of year.
Alcohol intake: See start of year.
Chronic Fatigue: Back to one hour's sleep a day – better than start of year.
Official handicap: 10.5
Rounds: 24
Average score: 16.04 over
Average score over last ten rounds: 11.8 over
Average score over last five rounds: 10.00 over
Eagles: 0
Longest drive: 277 yards (6 May, Lindfield, 18th)
Range balls hit: 4,800
Self-belief: 9/10
And the secret of golf is . . . buttering bread rolls.

1 August, Day 306: 59 to go.

I'm at the club, staring at my new identity. There, on the handicap listings, is Tony Lawrence. He's no longer a 24-handicapper, not even a 21.8. Nor is he a 7 or 8, mind you. He's 10.5.

I contemplate my new self. Is there any bitter after-taste,

considering James's prediction? It would have been fun to be awarded a single-figure handicap. But, hand on heart, I'd be an impostor. A single-figure handicapper, for me, is the genuine article. I have my moments, true. But they don't usually last eighteen holes. I can still top a drive and slice my next out of bounds. I'm still frightened of playing away from Lindfield. And, given the choice, I'd opt for the yellow tees. That's like having a big 'L' on your back.

James explains the committee's decision. There were several factors. There was the difficulty of the course and of the conditions. Most importantly, though, they felt a single-figure handicap had to be earned. That means scoring under pressure, in medal rounds and competitions.

If I really want a single-figure handicap – and let's be honest, the importance of 9 over 10 is merely a metric flattery – I'll surely get one. All I have to do is sign up for medal rounds. And find someone to look after Emma on Saturdays.

Yes, mere metric flattery . . . That said, I can't help noticing that my average score over the last five rounds is 10.00. It would be nice to dip under that.

The remaining goal, though, is Martin, Matthew and Roger. The Brothers' Match has been set for next month. It's the last of the main goals that I set myself ten months ago.

7.30 p.m. Everything's going to plan. Emma's in bed, on time, we've read our story and I'm by the door. She looks vaguely sleepy. I'm looking forward to an evening of The Golf Channel and buying golf books promising the world in seven days on Amazon . . . when a little voice suddenly enquires: 'Daddy, why do we swallow?'

7.35 p.m. Emma – totally awake – and I – suddenly weary – are in front of the laptop, reading about swallowing and saliva and parotid, sublingual and submandibular glands on the Internet. It's rather interesting, actually, but I can't help feeling that I've been had. Again.

7.58 p.m. Emma – in bed at last.

'Goodnight, Ems.'

'Daddy, I'm hungry.'

8.22 p.m. Emma's asleep, breadstick crumbs in her hair. After a bit of Internet surfing and The Golf Channel I read *The Secret of Golf*. According to a chap called Jimmy Ballard, it's all about connection. You have to imagine your upper biceps plugged into your torso. You hit the ball with a connected turn, not with your arms. Is that what Pharro's been saying? It seems so uncomfortable and fettered. That can't be right, surely? It's like swinging inside a straitjacket.

58 days to go: I pop my pills, then contact my solicitors – Pharro, Firkins and Malins. My golf lessons have become sporadic. To be honest, I'm questioning the point.

James is also sceptical. 'You've just shot the lowest scores of your life, you're going to have a bunch of lessons and they'll suggest you change something. That's what teachers do. But if it ain't broke, why fix it? Why not play with what you've got?'

I have no coherent reply. I suppose I just don't feel I've cracked it yet. Perhaps one never does. It's that inescapable idea of a perfect swing . . . I book the lessons and delve down the back of the sofa in search of coins.

57 days to go: I knew this would happen. Actually, I'm surprised it's taken this long. My left elbow's killing me. So is my left knee. And my back's sore from all the attempted toe-touching. I knew I'd get a golf injury if I made an effort.

Secretly, I'm rather impressed with myself. I thought my days of sporting injuries were long gone.

Doc does not understand why I'm so keen to reach my toes. She doesn't play golf. She says the elbow's tendonitis and that I should rest. No time. I'm into the last two months. Grin. Bear it.

'How are the anti-depressants going?' asks Doc.

'No change.'

'And the gym sessions?'

'Er . . .'

Some severe finger-wagging later and I head straight for the gym, where I fill in a questionnaire and receive a torture-chamber tour. I meet Bert – he's 80 and walks with a cane – and Ethel, who's had both hips replaced, is hard of hearing and relies on a stock reply of 'I'm sure you're right, dear'. Bert and Ethel are allowed to do five minutes on the bike and four on the cross trainer. I'm allowed to do three and two. Bert is to make sure I don't overdo things.

My personal trainer wants me in the gym three days a week. Snowballs in hell.

56 days to go: 9 a.m. Lindfield range. I continue the struggle with my new driver. If I could just hit 270 regularly, rather than 240 . . . Is this the missing piece of the jigsaw? If I could only drive, I'd be satisfied.

I practise Saunders and Nicholas chips, I try to butter rolls and I hit off Sanders' irregular lies. I attempt fades and draws. I mix things up. I hit off one leg and shut my eyes. Or am I overdoing the deliberate, varied practice thing? The ball goes everywhere.

10 a.m. I ask James to have a look at my driving. He brings

out an armoury of test clubs. He has a launch monitor and checks my swing speed. Result? I perplex him. I make no sense. I'm an enigma. My swing speed varies from 86 to 103mph. I have no clearly repeatable shot shape. No one can build a club for such variances, he mutters.

12 p.m. I go to the gym and cycle very slowly. Bert, a Tour de France yellow jersey by comparison, says hello. Ethel, polka-dot jersey (Queen of the Mountains), is sure I'm right.

55 days to go: Lesson with Malins. I tell him proudly about my new handicap.

He watches and says: 'Hm . . . '

My technique's not much improved despite everything, he argues. I've just learnt how to get round Lindfield, that's all. I examine the video. Nasty. There's a big slide right on the backswing, my hands are as low as ever and then there's a big tug and slide left. He tells me to tuck in my right foot and turn my upper body more against a stable lower body. In a fit of pique, I tell him I can't.

'It hurts my back,' I say. 'Heck, I'm nearly fifty.'

'Are you?' says Malins. 'I thought you were nearer forty.'

So I get something out of the lesson after all. Bright chap, Malins. I may be useless but at least I'm a young-looking useless. I make a mental note to tell Bert and Ethel. And I make a note to visit the osteopath.

54 days to go: Lesson with the Rottweiler, at Knightsbridge. Hugh Grant nowhere to be seen. Pharro says I'm too cramped. And using my arms as usual to compensate for my lack of turn.

'Address the ball,' he orders.

'Hello ball,' I say, laughing at my own joke.

Pharro doesn't. 'Look, your hands are next to your thighs. Push them further away.'

Pharro's quite pleased by the end. I leave with the same old swing thoughts — takeaway, wrist cock, much more shoulder turn. It's just a matter of glueing them together.

53 days to go: Lesson with Firkins, at Lindfield. My takeaway's better but my hands are floppy at the top. 'You're slapping,' he says. Is this another way to say disconnection? I suspect it is . . .

I stick to varied practice. At Burgess Hill range there's a sloping mat simulating downhill and uphill lies. Nobody ever uses it. I do. I lose my balance, fall off and jar my left knee again.

9 August, 52 days to go: Dad's deathday. Which is a funny way to put it. It makes it sound morbid. That's not how I feel.

It's five years now but seems like yesterday. I cried when I was phoned with the news — I was on a London bus, I recall — and I cried at the funeral. I was trying to give a eulogy at the time. Nobody understood a word.

Today though, I'm all smiles. I've nothing but good memories of Dad. That's a fair legacy. I'd be pleased with that, if I were him.

He comes back to me at the oddest of times. When I see somebody playing French cricket. Or boules on the beach. For me, Dad is Dutch gin. He's bicycle clips. He's Bristol, and baking bread on Sunday mornings, and crosswords and classical music. He's skimming stones. He's nightshirts, and gentleness, humanity and correct pronunciation. Five years on and Dad's still all pervasive.

Best of all, I still hear him. I hear him when I say 'daft hap'orth!' to Emma, just as he said 'daft hap'orth!' to me. I hear him saying 'Mrs L' to Mum. The other day I heard him laugh and realised that that, also, was me. Auntie Pat, Dad's sister, says that I'm the son that reminds her most of him. That makes me happy. If I grow increasingly like Dad I'll have done well enough. I could do without the flatulence, though.

I'm glad that Dad died, in retrospect. He'd had a bad stroke and was holed up in hospital. He wasn't coming back. He wouldn't have liked to linger on in those circumstances. So, for him, I'm glad. He always said he wouldn't make 'old bones'. I'm just sorry for us.

And I'm sorry for Mum. She's had the heart ripped out of her old life and that's not coming back either. She's not smiled a proper smile since, not one of those smiles that break out magically, like winter sun through cloud. The sort she wore at her wedding. And on Christmas mornings. And when, aged nine, I risked telling her a boarding-school joke about a tractor, a giraffe and hydraulics.

Life weighs heavily on Mum without Pops. She lives on the edge of a gaping hole. Sometimes I think they should have gone together. They were inter-connected. In the Greek myth, Baucis and Philemon are granted that wish by the gods. They die at exactly the same moment and are transformed into trees, their branches intertwining. I liked that story, at school, but now it makes me feel sad. Where are Zeus and Hermes when you need them?

Still. I'm glad Mum's here. She adds weight and stability to our lives. She gives us a past. I hope that's a comfort to her.

51 days to go: 11 a.m. 'Hi, Bert. Hi, Ethel!'

'I'm sure you're right, dear.'

'Don't overdo it, Tony.'

2 p.m. Lindfield Golf Club, an hour before Emma pick-up, and I notice a new photograph on the wall. It's Ronnie O'Sullivan, the world snooker champion, and a mate of his. Apparently O'Sullivan plays golf. Perhaps I could interview him, instead of Hugh Grant?

I look him up on the Internet. There's a newspaper article. O'Sullivan seems to have two contrasting sides – upbeat cheeky prodigy versus gloom-ridden introvert. He sounds a bit like me. Not the 'prodigy' bit. The 'gloomy' bit. I have ME to blame. He has genius.

'Once it becomes an obsession it can isolate you,' he says of his trade. 'And once you become isolated you become miserable.' I decide not to contact O'Sullivan. Grant's bound to be more cheerful.

7 p.m. I have another go at Delia Smith's broccoli soufflé. It's not half bad this time, if a little deflated. Emma refuses to have anything to do with it.

50 days to go: I pop my pills. I go to the gym. Stomach crunches and sit-ups. Touch my nose, flirt with my toes.

I play with James. I feel a bit weary. I go round in 14 over.

49 days to go: Pop pills. Gym. Play with Roger. Feel OK. Go round in 10 over.

48 days to go: Pills. Gym. Nose. Lose in a club competition to a nice chap called Noel. I play to 10, he to 6.

47 days to go: Text from James.

'Demo driver ready. Fancy a three-ball – 4 p.m.?'

4 p.m. The club, with 11.5 degrees of loft, looks fine but

feels weird. James has put extra weight in the grip. 'It's a hunch,' he says.

For the first time in months, I send out a soaring, high drive. I have another go and the same thing happens. It flies! Fantastic. But isn't this cheating? I can't hit a normal driver in the air but James has found a technological short-cut around my swing. Mess about with the weighting, add loft and hey presto. Oh well. Who am I to argue?

I play with James and the guy from the O'Sullivan photo. He turns out to be Pete Cohen, a sports psychologist.

Cohen opens with a piercing 270-yard drive down the 1st fairway. Another shot never to be forgotten. But I play well too. Actually, I play beautifully, relatively speaking. Then I realise I'm playing beautifully relatively speaking and Old Tom whispers on the 15th tee: 'All you need to do now is . . . ' I slash my four-iron out of bounds and blow the last three holes.

'You're still a good bloke,' says Cohen with a smile.

I play to 10.

45 days to go: I'm hiding in the corner of the gym. Sarah, one of the LBAALMFPMs (her daughter Ruby's with Emma in Copper Beech Class. Or is it Plum Class this year? Olive? Deadly Nightshade? Hemlock?), is pummelling her upper thighs on some contraption. Sarah is statuesque – 'don't call me Amazonian, Tony, that makes me sound muscular – and stop staring' – and ridiculously fit. She storms from machine to machine, pulling them off their hinges. She throws personal trainers across the room as part of her workout. I hide behind Ethel but Sarah spots me doing a 3.5kg bench press.

'Hi Tony! Fancy training together?'

Oh God. She'll kill me. Where's Bert when you need him?

40 days to go: Cohen agrees to a golf interview. I'm tempted to tell him, just as I told Surtees, that I don't really believe in his dark arts but Cohen pre-empts me.

'Psychology,' he tells me, 'is the biggest load of tosh.'

I think that must rate as the best opener to any interview I've ever carried out.

He goes on: 'Psyche means "being". So psychology is the analysis of your being. How can you do that? You can't. Where would it start and end?'

I find myself arguing for, rather than against: 'But psychology can surely help us to understand, and thus manage, our mind better?'

'Possibly,' he rejoins. 'But what's the mind? I see it as a joke. The biggest joke in the world.

'Yes, it does remarkable things, but it's also incredibly primitive. It does what it thinks it's supposed to do, based on practice and conditioning. That's why we clean our teeth every night and look before crossing a road. Your brain doesn't really know what's right and wrong, it just does. On a golf course, your brain does what it's done before. So if you normally duff shots and get frustrated, that's what your brain will help you to continue doing. It's been hard-wired.'

Wait a minute, wait a minute . . . but Cohen carries on.

'If a computer program goes wrong, you delete it. Why can't you do that with your mind – just delete negative thoughts? Because it's primitive, that's why. It's just a channel. If you channel your brain into worry, fear, anger and resentment, that's where it goes. And some people do that. Their minds hold them back.'

Blimey. Actually, that makes sense. There's your 'glass half-empty' brigade as well as the 'half-full', isn't there?

'Exactly. The human mind can create wonderful things, but it also creates illusions and fantasies. Lots of people labour with the feeling that they're not quite good enough in some way, that they don't quite fit in. But people aren't perfect. Nothing we do is perfect.

'People should give themselves more slack. Instead, they get in their own way. They go back to what they know, where they feel comfortable. Annika Sorenstam didn't win for two years after her first major. Why? She couldn't deal with the success. So she sabotaged herself.

'It's that other voice in our heads – Old Tom Morris, in your case. We get over-analytical. But think of your greatest moments in life. You were probably just enjoying, rather than analysing. Look at your daughter playing. She's in the moment. She's just being.'

Cohen is working with the Golf College students. He's built like a boxer. Having studied sports science, he began life as a physical instructor before making his name by writing a weight loss book. Psychology's now the name of his game, whether at Lindfield or with the likes of O'Sullivan or Tim Henman, another of his former pupils.

I ask him for the secret of golf, coupled with my 'why-don't-people-get-better' query, although I feel he's already answered that.

He comes back with a question of his own. How, he asks, did I improve?

Er . . . I waffle about rolling wrist, putting, course management. He cuts me short.

'I'll tell you what it was, Tony. You. You made the difference. And why? Because you wanted to. You had a goal and nothing was going to stop you. People who excel focus on something and do whatever it takes. Some are relentless. Others explore. You've explored, taking bits from different teachers. Who's to say that's not the right way? You've worked it out for yourself. You haven't used teachers as crutches. Believe me, many people do just that. What have you done? It's called self-discovery.'

'That makes sense,' I stammer, feeling suddenly very, very important. Gosh. It's me – I'm the secret of golf!

'It's more than sense, Tony. It's fact.'

A lot of what Cohen says I understand. He talks about being analytical at the right time, not when you're playing a shot. He talks about golf as rhythm and a transfer of energy. 'Care about short putts,' he says, 'but not worry over them.' Focus is the key, not hard work. I should observe without getting drawn into distracted thinking. (Henman, he says, was playing at Wimbledon once when he saw a man tottering through the crowd with a tray of beers. He hoped the man would not fall. 'Not the sort of thinking you need with Federer waiting on the other side of the net.')

But some of what he says loses me. It enchants me, but veers off towards the mystical.

'Golf is a reflection of how you are with yourself.'

Great! But I'm not too sure what it means.

'Golf gives you space.'

Great! Fantastic! Wow! What?

Cohen leaves the best to last.

He offers to help with my putting. He asks me to shut my eyes and concentrate on my breathing.

Who is my favourite putter? Tiger, I say.

'Right. Picture him. Watch his routine. See his every move. Imagine stepping inside his body. See through his eyes, hear what he hears. Be Tiger.'

A few minutes later and we're on the putting green. I get lost in the role. I normally crouch over my putts but now I'm standing taller. I find I'm putting with a more in-to-square-to-in stroke rather than my favoured straight-back-and-straight-through. I'm breaking all the rules I've established with Gilroy. Mechanically, considering my body type, I'm doing everything wrong. Except that the ball goes in the hole. Again and again. And when the ball does miss, I feel a mixture of amazement and indignation.

What the heck's going on?

Cohen smiles.

'It's a trick, Tony, just a trick. Psychology's a trick. I can tell you quite honestly, hand on heart, it has taught me nothing that has been of any long-term use. Mental techniques seem to work only for a very short time. Most people go back to what they know.

'Changing perspective is what it's all about. That's much harder to achieve.

'As for you, you've done what you set out to do. You can play golf. Just go out now and have fun. See where it takes you.'

Driving home, I realise that I am wearing black trousers and a red polo shirt. Tiger Woods's colours.

Well, if it is a trick, it's a bloody good one.

39 days to go: I'm practising at the range at Lindfield while being watched by blind Master Po, or, if you prefer, by Obi-Wan Kenobi. That's who the funny little man reminds me of, anyway. He's short, of Asian descent and wears a thick brown duffel coat and a quiet, barely perceptible smile. He hasn't yet spoken but I sense immediately that he's some sort of wise man, some kind of wizard. I don't hear him walk up. He just appears, and watches, and smiles, and says nothing. And I can tell you, it's hard to concentrate on hitting your seven-iron with Obi-Wan Kenobi watching you.

Blind Master Po, incidentally, was the Shaolin monk in the 1970s television series *Kung Fu* which I became addicted to as a child — Po was Grasshopper's teacher, for those of you ancient enough to remember — while Obi-Wan Kenobi was the hermitical Jedi Master played by Alec Guinness in *Star Wars*. Both were blessed with equal powers of insight and foresight.

'Hello,' I say.

And an hour later we're still talking. Or rather, he is. Grasshopper's doing the listening.

Obi-Wan Kenobi, it turns out, is a close friend of Pete Cohen. Actually, he's a bit more than a friend. A retired doctor, he's something of a mentor. A source of wisdom. A bedrock. I'm tempted to say he's the psychologist's psychologist. He's on a visit, with his wife. And he does have a name, which he shares readily. He'd just rather not have it mentioned in a book.

We start talking about seven-irons. Then I tell him about my challenge. I tell him how it's gone. The numbers are good, but I don't really feel I've quite got golf yet, 'if that makes sense'.

And he says: 'You have a pattern which identifies you as Tony. You have your own image of Tony. Your identity. You have created little boxes where Tony lives. You carry them everywhere with you, even though they are heavy.

'You're a victim of your own system, just as you are a victim of a society which identifies you by your driving licence and your social security number. So how do you let go? Why not say: "I am not Tony any more. I am a friend of Tony. The friend of Tony can do anything he wants. He says: 'When you need me, just call me.'"

'Your golf is just the same. You want to be in control, and so you are still frustrated. But you can't control golf. If you let all this go, you will have yourself. And you will have the game. There is no reward in struggling. Why bother? It's a choice you can make.'

And he says to me: 'You have improved your game over the past year and you have improved your life. But which came first?'

He tells me that golf holes are bigger on the far side. He tells me putting is about wanting to hole the ball. 'If you want to hole it the ball is already there.'

He explains that some people throw tantrums on the golf course because they are rediscovering the freedom of childhood. They are escaping the daily pressure of being responsible adults and the stress of their jobs and everyday lives. 'They are actually enjoying it, even if it does not look like it, they feel good about themselves – that is what human beings are.'

He says all kinds of things that are twice as mystical as Cohen and, again, I love the sound of what he says even when I struggle to make sense of it.

And he tells me how once he met a young struggling professional golfer from Ohio who, against all expectation, had qualified for the Open but had decided not to go. It clashed with his honeymoon and anyway, he said, he had never played links golf. He knew nothing about knockdown shots and all that strange Scottish stuff.

'But why don't you want to go?' Obi-Wan Kenobi asked him.

'I've just told you. It's because of my honeymoon, and because of the style of golf.'

'But why don't you want to go?'

So The Man From Ohio — ranked 396th in the world — stopped and thought, and then he said that, actually, honestly, he feared looking a fool on such a big stage.

But Obi-Wan Kenobi thought that, all things considered, a European honeymoon might be nice, wouldn't it? It would be different. And why not include the Open as part of the holiday? The Man From Ohio couldn't play links golf, so there would be no pressure. There'd be absolutely no expectation. He'd just go and play for fun and his new wife would enjoy the scenery and they'd have a ball.

And The Man From Ohio decided to take part after all. His local caddy — he did not have a regular caddy himself — helped him prepare by showing the best way to hit bump-and-runs with a three-wood. And The Man From Ohio began to play and experiment and have fun. And he loved every minute, right up to the point when they handed him the Claret Jug. The year was 2003 and the man's name was Ben Curtis.

And that is still the best golf story I've ever heard.

38 days to go: Jan, I and Emma go on holiday to a small, quiet caravan park overlooking the sea in Dorset. The rains falls but fails to spoil the view. Emma has her ice creams and her rock pools, Jan her locally-sourced food, morning newspapers, her sunsets and cream teas. I have my seven-iron. There's a golf club on the crest of the hill. I'm allowed odd visits. As long as I return with tubs of vanilla and the *Guardian*.

I sit back, in the quiet of the evening, and read *The Inner Game of Golf* by W. Timothy Gallwey. Gallwey's like Cohen and Obi-Wan Kenobi. I love what he says, even if I only understand half of it. There's a bit on Aikido, on balance and on centered power.

And I sit back and I read *Zen Golf* by Dr Joseph Parent, and there's some similar stuff. I knew it. I was right. Golf's a martial art.

And I sit back and, on a whim, I Google 'Aikido+martial arts+West Sussex'. Then I fire off some more emails into the dark.

32 days to go: 9.15 p.m. I'm sitting on a stack of punch bags in a Brighton kick-boxing centre, watching an Aikido training session.

Phil Rozier is confused by my email – he doesn't even play golf – but he invites me to observe a two-hour training session. I can leave at any time, he says, unconvinced. But I stay. And I'm utterly convinced. Aikido is the secret of golf.

You only have to set eyes on Rozier to get the point. I walk into the room and I identify the instructor immediately. It's not that he's 6ft 1in or 14½ stone. It's something about the way he stands. He looks heavily attached to the ground. He's solidly centred, yet at the same time on the verge of moving. It's hard to explain.

Rozier teaches his students blocks and feints and punches and throws. Power, he says, emanates from the centre. Slap a man to the chest with your arm and he won't move. Step into him with rotating hips and your arm connected to your body, however, and you'll walk right through him as if he weren't there. At least, that's what happens when Rozier does it. His willing students are sent flying in all directions. Then he demonstrates the difference between an arm-driven punch and a full-bodied punch. The first barely troubles a paper bag. The second leaves big dents in concrete walls.

So there it is again – the difference between short hooks

and long-armed slogs. It's also the difference between my golf swing and Els's. Well, one of them.

Afterwards, I ask Rozier about the source of his power.

'It's called "chi" or "dantien" in Chinese and "ki" or "hara" in Japanese but it's difficult to explain,' he says. 'One of the great masters told me recently in Japan that he'd been doing Aikido for sixty years but never heard a satisfactory explanation. Nobody can quite put their finger on it – perhaps that's why there are so many words for it.

'Some say it's an internal power, focused around your centre. Others say it's the strength that people produce in times of trauma – you know, when a granny lifts up a car to free her granddaughter. It's natural and doesn't need to be trained. It's just a matter of tapping into it.

'I know that makes it sound mystical. All I know is that it exists, and that Aikido helps find it.'

Rozier, an environmental consultant, discovered Aikido at university. He'd never been sporty but was soon training six times a week. He'd watched Kung Fu movies as a kid, and liked the thought of a black belt. 'I chose Aikido because it was so obscure and different.'

Learning Aikido, he says, takes years. 'People don't understand that. It's too much of a "now" culture. They don't want to work for anything. That's my personal gripe with society.'

His friends say he's a calm character. He's never had to use Aikido to get himself out of a tight spot. 'Not in the physical sense, anyway. I think you use it mentally more than anything else. A student of martial arts knows what damage can be inflicted on another person, so they avoid conflict if possible.'

I'm convinced at last. I have to turn my hips and my core

and my shoulders, not swat with my arms. I'll try harder to get the hang of it.

As for Rozier, he should take up golf. He'd make mincemeat of it.

31 days to go: I try to make an acquaintance with my 'chi' in the gym. I do some stomach crunches. I feel impressive. I pose in front of the mirror and fancy I look just like an Aikido grand master. Bert comes up and winks.

'I get constipation too,' he whispers.

SEVENTEEN

CHIHUAHUAS AND BAZOOKAS

'You've just one problem. You stand too close to the ball after you've hit it'

—*Sam Snead*

Weight: Not good, but too late to care now.
Waist measurement: Too late.
Diet: Perhaps it's genetic?
Alcohol intake: Definitely genetic.
Chronic Fatigue: 45 minutes a day!
Official handicap: 10.5
Rounds: 28
Average score: 15.321 over
Average score over last ten rounds: 11.0 over
Average score over last five rounds: 9.8 over
Eagles: 0
Range balls: 5,400
Longest drive: 277 yards (6 May, Lindfield, 18th)
Self-belief: 8/10
And the secret of golf is . . . You. And Aikido.

1 September, 29 days to go: 7.30 a.m. It's 26 days to The Brothers' Match. The final sprint. Keep Martin, Matthew and Roger in my sights. Don't flag.

7.31 a.m. Me (shouting): 'Emma, breakfast! Porridge!'
Emma (faintly, upstairs): 'Bother!'
Emma (loudly, downstairs now): 'Can I have Frosties instead?'
Me: 'No.'

'Chocolate spread?'

'No.'

'Is there a treat in my lunch box?'

'No.'

'Can I watch TV?'

'No.'

Emma: 'I wish adults would say yes sometimes.'

8.00 a.m. 'Emma, do your hair, teeth, spell "neighbour", where's your cardigan, look at the state of your room, what's 93 minus 45, coat, coat, no, the pink one, let's go, come on, come on, we'll be late, I'm waiting, I'm waiting...'

9.30 a.m. I stand on the gym scales and blink. There's no denying it – 13st 10lb. I lost a bit of weight and now it's all back on. The whole bloody lot.

It's odd. I'm going to the gym regularly enough. I'm still doing my Harris workouts. The trouble is, I visit the biscuit tin just as often. Despite Jan's best efforts, I still eat expansively and erratically.

Just as oddly, though, I'm feeling pretty good about life. Actually, I'm feeling very good. I feel I've got more energy than I've had for years.

Remember that film *Awakenings*, about patients roused from a catatonic state by some wonder drug? I feel a bit like that. Perhaps I really was depressed? I vow to continue popping pills and gyming it. Not that I enjoy it. If I enjoy gyms at all, it's in the past tense. I enjoy having gone.

Perhaps I'll ask Cohen about his weight-loss book.

And perhaps I won't.

11.00 a.m.: I'm signing up for Saturday's club medal and it strikes me. My last five Lindfield rounds read 5, 14, 10, 10, 10 – that's an average of 9.8 over!

27 days to go: 4.45 a.m. Emma wakes. She's had a bad dream so we scrunch it up into a ball, open her bedroom window and throw it out. Then I cuddle her back to sleep. I, though, remain wide awake, wondering whether you can scrunch up bad golf shots and throw them away. Or do they stay with you for ever, making you wake with a start in the middle of the night?

I go and surf the Internet. And I stumble across the 'Long Drivers of Europe'.

Apparently, I learn, there exist competitions in which the sole object is to monster the ball as far as possible. Mitch's sort of thing. My driving's still a weakness. I should contact them.

I look out of the window and see Next-Door Frank rolling down the hill towards the station. Frank has a knack of looking as windblown and unkempt in a suit and tie as he does in his weekend togs. I thought civil servants were pristinely presented until I met Frank. You cannot but warm to the man.

25 days to go: The second – and last – medal of my year proves amusingly eventful. It shows how far I've come. And how far I have to go, to be a proper golfer.

I take it very, very seriously. I clean my clubs. I warm up. I visualise. I focus. And I'm disqualified on the 1st green, on the 4th tee and on the 9th fairway.

Otherwise, things go rather well.

I stand on the 1st tee and feel queasy. It's not nerves. It's having to behave. This is an official event, heavy on etiquette. I smile invitingly at my partners. Invitation declined. I feel as relaxed as an iron bar.

As the lowest handicapper, I drive off first. I do just fine. I get on in regulation but miss a 4-footer for par. The ball teeters on the edge. Disgusted and without thinking, I flick the ball up into my hand with my putter.

'You're disqualified,' says the senior member of our party. 'Failing to hole out. Rule XB379AQDC 41229, subsection PZW, clause (iii) [sic].'

The woman-who-shall-remain-nameless (she'd be drummed out of Lindfield if ever identified) then realises, however, what she's dealing with — a would-be, clueless golfer. Her mothering side surfaces. We'll pretend it didn't happen. I'm not to say anything to anyone. Against the rules and all her golfing instincts, she re-qualifies me.

On the 4th, I ask a fellow competitor if the hole is on the top or bottom tier of the green. Oops. 'Rule ZPZ12RFC etc etc . . . ' On the 9th, I clip a stray practice ball back on to the range. 'That could be construed as practising during a hole.' Blimey. You need a law degree to negotiate eighteen holes safely.

Otherwise, I play nicely and, pretending to be Tiger, I putt beautifully. I hole three 12-footers, chip in from 50 feet, get the first back-to-back birdies of my life, produce my longest drive ever of 295 yards (admittedly downhill and with James's cheating club) and I come second overall on 8 over par (a 24-handicapper wins the medal, playing to 17. In the bar, he complains bitterly that his handicap will be cut. I wish Saunders had been there to witness it).

Two days later I'm cut to 10.3. If I'd played to 6, and not driven into the trees on the 15th, I'd have crept into singles. But it's a fantastic way to finish the year. From 24 to 10.3. I'll take that.

Now for The Brothers.

5 p.m. I'm taking Jan and Emma through my scorecard, shot by shot (Jan hides behind her newspaper, Emma amongst

her retinue of Barbies), when the phone rings. It's the Long Drivers of Europe. Have they just heard about my 295-yarder? Do they want to sign me up? No. But they do give me Adam 'Stinger' Stacey's contact details.

18 days to go: I meet 'Stinger'.

Now I'm not one for nicknames. Never have been, never will. That's just me. But I make an exception here. 'Stinger' can have all the nicknames he wants.

I make the allowance within ten minutes of shaking Stacey's hand. As well as the interview, he offers me a lesson. But he needs 'a few taps' to warm up first.

The range is 300 yards long, with a fence at the far end. Stacey yawns, stretches and makes a half-swing.

I've replayed the image in my mind a thousand times. That's all it was. A smooth, leisurely half-swing. A tap. And the ball, defying each and every one of Newton's Laws, punches into the fence on the fly.

I try to say something but I can't breathe. I knew what to expect. I'd mugged up on Stacey's 2005 World Long Drive Championship exploits. But this is reality. It's the single most awe-inspiring thing that I've ever seen. Involving a golf ball, anyway.

Until, that is, drive number four clears the fence. The golf course lies beyond the range, so Stacey checks that the fairway's clear. His longest drive lands at around 380 yards – but it's a chilly day, he explains, and they are, after all, only range balls.

His best strike in an official competition is 462 yards. That's a quarter of a mile. Four lengths of Manchester United's Old Trafford football pitch. As Ian Baker-Finch once said of John

Daly's driving: 'I don't go that far on my holidays.' The only way to hit that far is by teeing off and running backwards.

So 'Stinger' it is.

My turn. I feel like a Chihuahua in a Great Dane's shadow. I don't reach the back fence. I probably wouldn't even reach a front fence. I swing manically but Newton's Laws are back in force.

I don't know why I've always been a poor driver, but I have a theory. Actually, Cohen has a theory and I'm appropriating it.

I try too hard. Or rather, I rely on violence.

Cohen says it goes back to when Homo sapiens first picked up a stick with assault, battery and lunch on their mind. Sticks were for killing. Give a man a club and a ball and he'll revert to his most primitive incarnation. ('What, you know Mitch?' I say.) On Sundays, though, Man took a break from beating mammoths to death. He resorted to bashing inanimate objects. For fun. Thus golf.

Today's highly engineered drivers bear little resemblance to sticks. They're bazookas. I seem to spend most of my time shooting myself in the foot with mine, I tell Stacey. I see mammoths everywhere, I think 'kill!' and I blast out of bounds.

He advises me to lean further away from the target and to stay longer on my right side in the downswing. 'Don't sway, turn.' There's no immediate improvement.

Stacey's story is as dramatic as his ball striking.

His rise to fame was largely accidental. Indeed, it began with just that – an accident. Followed by knee surgery. Nine months later, he was competing in Las Vegas against the best sluggers around.

'Yes, it was a crazy year,' concedes Stacey. 'I was studying to become a PGA golf professional when I ruptured my cruciate knee ligament playing football. That meant no golf for months.

'I was furious. I limped to the range, intent on smashing up my clubs. I couldn't put any weight on my right leg, so I belted some balls using my upper body, forearms and wrists. Surprisingly, I hit the ball OK. I started tweaking.

'Then it happened. I lined up this shot, and flushed it . . . 300 yards, dead straight.

'I just stood and stared. I'd only ever hit 10 or 20 yards further than that in my whole life! But then I ripped the next ball out there too. I was finding clubhead speed that I'd never had before. Normally, using your hands and arms is erratic. But I was dropping the club on the inside, whipping my hands through and absolutely tearing into it. I'd never attempted anything like it before. It was weird.'

Things would soon get weirder.

Stacey, still rehabilitating, visited the London Golf Show with some mates and came across a driving simulator. Have a bash, read the challenge, and the best can go head-to-head with two European long drive champions. Beat them – which, of course, you won't in a year of Sundays – and win yourself a new driver.

Egged on, Stacey had a bash. The simulator gave him 320 yards. Then, helped by a few bottles of beer – 'nine, actually' – he forgot all about it.

Until the group passed the simulator again on their way out. And there he was. Adam Stacey. Still on the leaderboard.

'So I got the guys to hang around until the end. There were these two Swedish driving champions standing there. I'm 6ft 1in and weighed 14 stone at the time. They were colossal – 18 stone or thereabouts, 6ft 5in and twice as wide as me. I asked one of them if I could borrow his glove and got a pitying look back.

'Anyway, I stepped back into the simulator and blitzed it 338 yards. The first Swede managed 322 and stormed off. I beat the other one, too. My mates loved it. Then this bloke came up and asked if I'd ever considered entering long drive competitions. As for the driver I won, that went straight on eBay.'

A few months later, Stacey and his retinue were piling back into their cars for another lads' weekend.

'I got invited to this event in Scotland on the back of the London Golf Show. We drove up overnight, then went out for a drink the next evening. I took it easy, though. By then I'd realised it wasn't a Mickey Mouse competition. In fact, the top five qualified for the European championship.

'I wasn't exactly taking it seriously but I didn't want to look like an idiot. I hadn't done any particular practice but I could load up on my knee by then. By mixing my normal swing with my new arm-and-hand technique, I could now hit about 350.

'So we pitched up at St Andrews Bay, me clinging to my Titleist 9.5-degree, 44-inch driver. The twenty other guys taking part all knew each other. Nobody had a clue who I was, except for the Swedes. Their clubs were 50 inches long, brightly coloured and with odd brand names, and some of them had lofts as low as four, or even two degrees. That's less than a putter.

'There was this long straight grid, around 30 to 50 yards wide. You get split into groups. Each round, you get two minutes and forty-five seconds to hit six balls. The longest counts, the bottom half of each group gets eliminated, then you start again from scratch.

'There were about 100 spectators. I was a bit nervous but I held my own. There was a strong wind but I was hitting about 290 and reached the six-man final. I was first up. The wind picked up but I got another good one out. The next guy OB'ed all six. It dawned on me – my God, I'd qualified for the Europeans! I finished second overall.'

Stacey, of course, is not your average hacker. He's a natural sportsman, extremely flexible 'which is really important' and a former British schools gymnast champion. He's a top trampolinist and a useful cricketer and footballer. He took up golf aged ten and began with a handicap of 27. Five years later he was playing off 1.

After his Scottish surprise, Stacey contacted a specialist manufacturer and got hold of a 6-degree driver. He struggled. 'It was like a poker. The shaft only begins to kick at 135mph. My first effort got 4 foot off the ground and went sharp right.' After a few weeks, however, things clicked.

By the Europeans, he was surpassing 400 yards and qualified comfortably for the World finals in Mequite, Las Vegas, five weeks later.

By now he was someone. He'd earned his nickname. His flight, hotel and entry fee were paid by sponsors. But he still came across as a famine victim – relatively speaking – in the competitors' group photograph.

'Some of them looked like they'd come down from the mountains. God knows what they feed them on. Jason Zuback, the five-times world champion, had forearms the size of my thighs. There were professional golfers, ex-baseball stars and ice hockey players. Some of the swings, though, looked a bit ropey.'

The show, in the Virgin Mountain foothills of the Nevada

desert, rivals a professional tour event. The competition area is surrounded by stands for 4,000 spectators. There's ESPN, a 30x30ft television screen and hordes of autograph hunters. And there's a first prize of $100,000. Plus bonuses. Plus sponsorship deal.

Stacey progressed quietly through the preliminaries before firing a 383-yard howitzer. The 'Rookie of the Year' was in the final, barely six months after taking up the sport.

'By now it's late evening, under floodlights. I go last, with 377 to beat. I really think I can win. I smash my first ball straight down the tube and scream after it. There's a huge cheer. But the temperature has plummeted. It goes 350. I manage 367 with my fifth, and 360 with my sixth but no more.

'Then they announce the result: " . . . and in third place, 'Stinger' Stacey of England!" I've only gone and won $30,000! We go to The Strip that night. I want to place all my winnings on red at the roulette table but my girlfriend's having none of it. And that was it, my first year as a long driver. Un-bleedin'-believable.'

Stacey still hopes to play golf professionally. In the meantime, he works as a club pro. And enters long drive events. He's also a pro-am celebrity. 'If I stick to a two-iron and my conventional swing, I can get around in 65, but they want me to use my special driver, so I can just as easily score 81,' he smiles.

'But that's what it's about. Ask people at a range. They want to hit further.'

So why haven't handicaps come down, Stinger? Is it because most of us are Chihuahuas? No, apparently.

'Joe Public only finds an hour a week to practise, which isn't easy. You have to hit a lot of balls. You also need lessons. Most people are scared of lessons. They say they're too old to learn. Rubbish. You're never too old.'

I can't resist one more question.

'Can you hit it further than Tiger Woods?'

There's not even a suggestion of a pause.

'Without breaking sweat.'

14 days to go: I play with my neighbour Andy. Actually, Andy doesn't really play. He plays when his boss tells him to. He loses eight balls but finds one and is delighted. I hit averagely but scramble very nicely for 9 over.

On the elevated 15th tee, 'Chihuahua' Lawrence pretends to be 'Stinger' Stacey, leans away from the target, loads up his right side and loses his ball into the trees.

13 days to go: I'll never quite understand women.

I walk back from school with one of the LBAALMFPMs. She's feisty and fun and not obsessed with her children's latest spelling test. We indulge in banter. Most days she calls me 'grumpy', 'old', or 'git'. Some days she calls me all three together. I'm feeling pretty feisty myself this morning so I respond with a jest of my own. I suggest a school picture of her drawn by her daughter is inaccurate. The figure in the picture's too slim. Ha ha ha!

Mrs X's face turns to stone.

Gentlemen, this is a no-no. Do not joke about women's weight. Ever. Don't ask me why. It's off limits, that's all. They're allowed to call us grumpy, and old, and git and we must guffaw with amusement. But woe betide he who jests about the odd extra calorie.

I love women dearly but I'll never understand the rules. I'll always be a playground outsider.

I change the subject.

'That's a nice blue coat.'

'It's not blue, it's petrol,' she snaps back.

We pass a small field. There's a pig in it.

'Oh look, it's me,' says Mrs X, bitterly.

'It's a very nice shade of petrol,' I say, trying to regain lost ground. 'Your coat, I mean. Not the pig.'

'So are you saying I'm fat?' she replies.

We part, frostily.

Petrol? Petrol's black, surely? I'll never understand.

10 days to go: It's seven days to The Brothers' Match, ten days of my year remaining: I'm clutching at straws now, looking for anything to give me an edge. There are clubs all over the house. Even in the toilets (have you ever tried to swing a three-wood in a toilet? While sitting? It can be done, actually). There's my putting mat across the kitchen floor. I putt feverishly while over-cooking.

I watch TV and there is French golfer Raphael Jacquelin, possibly the most languid striker of a ball who has ever lived. He's not like Stacey — he's made of chicken wire rather than muscle — and looks like he's swinging at half pace while still giving the ball a healthy smack. How the hell does he do that? I phone up a journalist friend and ask for Jacquelin's phone number. He hasn't got it, but knows a man who might.

9 days to go: I head for Lindfield and there, in the clubhouse, is Denis Pugh, Colin Montgomerie's coach. He's instructing the College students.

I grab the chance, introduce myself, explain my golf challenge and ask him for two minutes of his time.

'Fire away,' he says.

I fire. Why haven't average handicaps improved?

Pugh seems nonplussed.

'Good question! Give me a few seconds to think that over – I'd like to give you a proper answer.'

When you deal with the Montgomeries of this world, I don't suppose average handicaps concern you overly. But Pugh frowns, ponders, and concludes that merely playing is not enough. And neither are lessons. It's the work in between which counts.

'People practise, but not enough,' he says.

The secret of golf – from a leading coach! It feels like Christmas! It must be my lucky day, I decide. So, that evening, I phone a number I've just been emailed.

To my consternation, Jacquelin answers.

'Hello, bonjour, guten Tag, hasta la vista,' I bluster, momentarily caught off guard. 'Je parlais avec Denis Pugh ce matin . . . '

Jacquelin proves to be an absolute gentleman and chats amiably away.

For him, golf's all about the basics.

'People don't want to be told that, but I see so many players who are all over the place. Their alignment's so bad, they don't know where they're aiming. They try to cut corners and they believe in magic secrets but there aren't any.'

I'm not sure this is what I want to hear. At least, I plead, give me the secret of your driving. You hit without apparent effort – you look like a slow-motion action replay for goodness sake – only for the ball to fly 300-plus yards. I've got less than a week left. I know Stinger's secrets — now tell me yours. Jeez, I swing my putter quicker than you swing your driver!

Jacquelin laughs.

'Yes, I know, I watch myself on television and it does look like I'm swinging slowly. But focus on my hips and you'll see they're moving pretty quickly. I'd say I'm at 80 per cent. It's all about the speed of the clubhead. That comes from rotation.

'I suppose I average about 260 metres (285 yards) but the key's staying on the fairway. I could go further, but my technique would suffer. That's what you should concentrate on. And I stick to my natural tempo. It's the same tempo I use with my seven-iron.'

8 days to go: Five days to go to The Brothers: A round with James. Stacey or Jacquelin, Stacey or Jacquelin? I'll try to do what Stacey told me while concentrating on Jacquelin's tempo. I can't do Stacey's tempo anyway. My spine would shatter into a thousand pieces. I hum 'Jacqu . . . e . . . lin' as I swing.

I play to 4 over par, my best ever.

I hit eight fairways out of fourteen and nine greens in regulation. There are two birdies. The chipping's solid. My game's not spectacular, just all-round decent, with a couple of long putts and a couple of lucky bounces off trees. I'm not doing cartwheels, but I'm well chuffed.

James's game, meanwhile, has gone to pot. He can't wait for the end of my year. He's convinced I've jinxed him. 'Dammit, you've got better and I'm going backwards! And stop bloody humming "Jackanory" whenever you hit the ball.'

6 days to go: Three days until The Brothers. I'm in Knightsbridge and Hugh Grant, yet again, is not. How can two people spend so much time in the same place without running into each other? It's uncanny. I'd texted Pharro, who said Grant was due in. So I rushed to London, sprinted out of the Tube and waved at Tim, Emma's big-hat, small-world doorman, as I dashed past. I'm 200 yards from the golf school, and only slightly purple-veined, and I get a text. From Pharro.

'Sorry! Cock-up. HG in next week.'

But next week's too late. Hugh and I, it transpires, are not to become golfing buddies after all. I will not be attending the launch of his next film. I'll never discover what Liz Hurley's really like. Enough's enough. Stalking's too time consuming. I can no longer justify the train fares.

I make do with a lesson.

And while Pharro and I are discussing something – rolling wrists, presumably, and a deeper turn – I spot a furtive movement out of the corner of my eye. It's Wilkinson, his back against the wall, slip-sliding as silently and unobtrusively as possible down the corridor. He's in camouflage, his trousers and shirt matching the colour of the wall paint. He stops, freezes and stares like a hunted animal, realising he's been spotted.

But I hesitate. Wilkinson, after all, isn't Hugh Grant. He's not even a poor man's Hugh Grant. Frankly, he's not even a penniless man's Hugh. He wears oddly patterned shirts and Christmas-present jumpers and wouldn't say boo to a gosling.

But he's a golf guru. And I haven't interviewed him yet. And, with seventy-two hours to the biggest match of the year, beggars can't be choosers.

But still I hesitate. I mean, it won't be much of an exchange. Wilkinson rarely says anything. And when he does, it's a hesitant, apologetic, indecipherable mumble.

But still. Against my better judgement, I dash out, rugby-tackle him and pin him to the floor. And I say: 'Dave, just a couple of minutes?'

He mumbles indecipherably. Probably something along the lines of: 'No, so very sorry, can't, got a lesson, I need to go shopping, absolutely not, must go home immediately, the ironing needs doing, I've left the bathroom light on . . . '

I frog-march him to the nearest chair. And I ask why handicaps haven't improved. And an extraordinary thing happens.

Dave Wilkinson Mark I suddenly transmogrifies into Dave Wilkinson Mark II. The man starts to talk. In full sentences. He starts waving his arms about almost as much as Gould, and he's almost as Rottweiler-forceful as Pharro. A fire blazes in his soul. I'd have been less surprised if he'd ripped his shirt off and turned into The Hulk.

Not that it's an assured start. I ask him his age. 'Er . . . fifty-five . . . no, fifty-six . . . actually fifty-eight, I think. Probably. Possibly. What year is it? When was I born?'

But then we get on to golf.

Wilkinson came to Knightsbridge Golf School for an afternoon lesson in 1970 and never left.

An aspiring professional, he wanted to play on tour but distrusted his swing. He'd consulted several teachers, always to the same refrain: 'Don't touch it, it's fine, it works.'

But he remained unhappy. Sure, he could score 65s, even a 63 on a very good day. There were the bad days too, though.

So he visited Leslie King, and he hit one ball, and the great man raised an eyebrow and said: 'Awful. Horrible. You have to start again.'

'It may sound odd but I was relieved,' says Wilkinson. 'I saw a way forward.'

'Mr King didn't, by any chance, use the word "crap"?' I interrupt.

'Heavens, no,' says Wilkinson. 'He was a straight talker, but he was also a gentleman.'

I make a mental note to discuss this with Pharro.

Nobody knew much about golf forty years ago, according to Wilkinson. There was no video analysis. You could either play or you couldn't. You copied the top players as best you could.

King, though, had a concept, and one convincing enough to attract top English amateurs and professionals.

'We all had terrible body turns in those days. We tilted – some people even taught shoulder tilt – and compensated with our hands. One in 1,000 might stumble on a good swing. It was like natural selection. But here was a man who explained the swing. He had the whole picture, not just bits and pieces. It was a revelation.'

King took two years to rebuild Wilkinson. He also gave him a job. A job of a lifetime. When King passed away, Wilkinson and Gould continued – and continue still – to spread the word.

Wilkinson gets historical. He talks about Faldo's massive influence. He turns philosophical. He talks about golfers' tendency to regress into bad, old habits 'as if they have a virus'. He gets technical. He discusses wrist supination.

Miracle of miracles, I understand what he says. He explains club release and – perhaps for the very first time – I understand that too.

I'm rapt. What about my old chestnuts, though – the secret of golf and those stubbornly high handicaps?

'The secret's knowing how to build a swing shape,' says Wilkinson. 'Once you know, you have it for life. The real secret's knowing what you're trying to do structurally. The wrist is crucial but you have to know the hand action at every point of the swing. We call it the hand line – the arc they follow, how they hinge, respond, and release the club. It's the thing most people miss.

'As for high handicaps, well, there's simply too much information on offer today. Most of it may be correct but it has no context. You need a complete model of the swing to avoid confusion.

'Imitation's not enough. Children imitate wonderfully. Adults don't. You have to be taught. And there aren't many really able teachers. They show you, but there's not quite enough information or detail for you to achieve it.

'Some people can play to a high standard despite a suspect technique, if they have great hand-to-eye co-ordination. But the average player won't get away with it. Remember Lee Trevino? One in a million! He took the club outside, then dropped it back on to a perfect line and elongated the impact area by sliding through the ball and holding off his wrist. It wasn't conventional, but it was beautiful. He was so good that, at the time, people thought it would become the way to play. Even Nicklaus did. The trouble was, nobody else could do it.'

I ask Wilkinson about Hugh Grant. I figure that this is the closest I'll ever get to him.

It turns out Grant was once almost as bad as I am – and with an identical flaw.

'He really rolled his hands, whipping the club behind him. That set off a series of compensations,' recalls Wilkinson. 'It was shockingly bad, but easy to fix. We did it within two years.'

Grant, though, then went his own way, hoovering up advice from every pro and fellow celebrity he met. His game duly disintegrated and he returned for a Knightsbridge detox.

'He'd wrecked the whole technical basis of his game. It looked almost impossible to get back. But he's managed it. He's good off the ball again, and slightly stronger in other ways, but still not quite stabilised at the top. You can play with that, but you're always on a knife edge. We're working on it. He's a 5-handicapper but wants to get down so that, on a good day, he can play to scratch. That's his ambition.'

My time's up.

'Do you still play, Dave?' I ask as he gets up.

No, he doesn't. He's too busy teaching. He gets his pleasure from his students.

'They phone you up, they get such a kick from it. To be honest, I don't miss the game. I'd rather practise striking the ball.'

What, just hitting in the net?

'Yes. It's the beauty of the shot-making that captivates me, you see. There's no other sport like it, where you can hit the ball so purely and powerfully. The feeling's awe-inspiring.

'I shouldn't say this, but the short game bores me. I know it's the key to scoring. But I'm obsessed with shot-making. My score doesn't bother me. Golf's ultimate test, for me, is how well you can drive.'

I feel as if I've been slapped in the face.

'Wow! Dave! You're the first . . . ' I blurt out.

But he really must go. So sorry. Another time, perhaps. In twenty years, say. The camouflage is back on. Wilkinson Mark II has left the building and I'm left with his alter-ego, a polite, softly spoken, sweetly smiling man who'd rather have his spleen removed than consider anything approaching a conversation.

A word of advice. If you want to be inspired about golf, go to Knightsbridge and talk to Dave Wilkinson. But first you'll have to spot him creeping along the corridor, haul him down, kneel on his shoulder blades and refuse to take no for an answer.

I took no for too long. I thought I wanted to talk to Hugh Grant. And all the time I was chasing false gods. Who needs an actor when you can have the real thing?

'Thanks again, Dave,' I say. 'Brilliant.'

He nods sheepishly, and shrugs, and mumbles something indecipherable. About a bathroom light having been left on, I think.

3 days to go: One day until The Brothers. I'm clearing the house of golf clubs, balls, gloves, tees and yellowing scorecards. Jan says enough is enough. It's high time we got back to normal. She asks me to clear the kitchen of my golf notes, and diagrams, and photos, leaflets, books, videos and training aids. She's very reasonable about it, considering. It's just that she'd like her old life back now, thank you very much. As well as the kitchen.

And I leaf through my golf challenge diary and I find, written on the very first page: 'I pledge to play one round – no, make that two, to prove the point – in single figures. Off the yellow tees. And drive a ball 300 yards (downhill and downwind along Tarmac, if necessary). And get an eagle. And beat my three brothers. Oh, and lose weight.'

I've never got an eagle, I've never driven 300 yards, and I never really lost any weight – not without the help of the 'flu. I cannot speak Spanish either, nor play the guitar. Oh, and I never got to meet Hugh Grant.

But I've managed to tick off the rest of my 'Things to Do' list. I even managed my two 75s off the whites, not the yellows. I'm not Ernie Els but the wildebeest is looking less absurd than he once did.

I also feel a lot better, both physically and mentally. I'm sleeping far less in the day. I'm not quite back to where I'd like to be – my failure to control the biscuits and red wine and my rapidly dwindling interest in the gym may not have helped – but I think there may be some life in the old dog after all. I can touch my toes too, occasionally. As long as I face uphill.

Did golf cure my Post-Viral Fatigue and the Male Midlife Crisis? No, of course not. But I'm sure it helped in some mysterious way.

There have been other bonuses too. Emma, despite the daily complaints about my insistence on homework, piano practice and a tidy bedroom, still calls out 'Daddy!' in the middle of the night whenever she has nightmares. Sometimes during the day, when she's particularly distracted or I'm doing particularly well, she even calls me 'Mummy'. It doesn't get better than that.

Oh, and there were those two questions, of course. Why have average handicaps failed to come down? And is there a secret?

To my own satisfaction at least, I've answered the first of them.

Sure, golf's difficult. 'Reverse every natural instinct and do the opposite of what you are inclined to do,' Hogan said, 'and you will probably come very close to having a perfect golf swing.'

But I still think it's not as hard as we choose to make it.

I believe that handicaps have not budged because so many golfers do not really want to improve. They just say they do. They may even manage to convince themselves that they do. But they see themselves in fairground mirrors. They believe in fairies and elves, they believe what they're sold, they chase false gods and place their trust in three-minute fixes. For many of us, it's the story of our lives. Yes, golf really does reflect us.

Or, as the philosopher Eric Hoffer argued, most people prefer excuses to achievements, because excuses can comfortably last a lifetime.

As for the secret of golf? Don't ask me. I haven't got a clue. It may have something to do with too much wrist roll and not enough shoulder turn, the short game, your lack of abdominal muscles, your lack of connection, your faulty attractors, your misguided acceleration after impact or your rubbish set of clubs. Who knows? Let's just say the experts disagree.

EIGHTEEN

THE BROTHERS' MATCH

'Any man can be a father. It takes someone special to be a Dad'

— author unknown

'Our siblings. They resemble us just enough to make all their differences confusing, and no matter what we choose to make of this, we are cast in relation to them our whole lives long'

— Susan Scarf Merrell

Weight: Just right, for somebody who's 7ft 1in tall.
Waist measurement: To be dealt with next year.
Diet: See above.
Alcohol intake: 61 million Frenchmen (and women) can't be wrong.
Chronic Fatigue: 45 minutes a day!
Official handicap: 10.3
Rounds: 31
Average score: 14.56 over
Average score over last ten rounds: 8.4 over
Average score over last five rounds: 8.2 over
Eagles: 0
Range balls: 6,100
Longest drive: 295 yards (5 September, Lindfield, 6th hole)
Self-belief: 9.5/10
And the secret of golf is . . . your guess is as good as mine.

27 September – The Big Day. The Brothers' Match. This is what it's all about.

Alarm 7 a.m. Jan's dealing with Emma this morning. I sneak downstairs and nothing stirs in the house.

Typical. My day off and Emma's still sound asleep. My day on and she'd have been awake at 5.30, looking for a pillow fight or an argument.

Porridge, with blueberries and nuts for slow-release energy. I clean my clubs and scrub the grips over breakfast. Which is probably why the porridge tastes of rubber. I brush my shoes and mark four balls with a putting alignment mark and TL1, TL2, TL3 and TL4. I think about marking a fifth but decide that would be defeatist. I iron my golf trousers and comb my hair, because Dad would have told me to.

We're to tee off at 11 a.m. I leave home at 8.30 a.m. and reach Burhill an hour later, giving me more than enough time to warm up and get used to the greens. I wonder how much time professionals give themselves? I hide the car, as usual, by the tradesman's entrance.

One by one, Martin, Matthew and Roger roll in.

We're an odd foursome. We couldn't be more different. Martin's all cerebral, I'm all talk, Matthew's all looks and Roger's all heart on his sleeve. We like different things just look at our wives. We've followed diverging paths only to end up within an hour's drive of each other. We love each other, in our own ways, but I'm not sure we'd be friends by choice, not all of us anyway. Blood being thicker than water, I'd jump under a train for each of them, but I'd be complaining loudly as I did so.

Roger, as my Lindfield neighbour, knows what I have planned. He knows what I've put myself through and he knows I'm here to win. Martin and Matthew have no clue what I've been up to for the past 362 days. I'm out to amaze them. The last time we played I was a hacker. The last time I played Martin I went down by six shots. They won't know what's hit them. I've also decided, as an extra, to try to record the first single-figure handicap score in the history of The Brothers' Match.

Matthew — the only one of us ever to have got close to mastering the game — announces he hasn't played for ages and requests a 24 handicap. Martin chokes uncontrollably and Roger and I steal a smile. And I think of Saunders and smile some more. And Matthew, really, honestly, naively can't see what the fuss is about.

By the 5th hole he's 1 over par, leading the field and Martin, red-faced with indignation, is convening an emergency meeting of the Handicap Committee. Matthew offers to go down to 20, which Martin still thinks is a cheek, and the two chunter on about it throughout the rest of the round.

Martin, I'm told, is highly competitive and ruthlessly ambitious but I can never see it. He must be quietly, intro-vertedly highly competitive, and so very gently ruthless. Nobody is more competitive than me today, though. I'm taking things super-seriously. I'm concentrating on each and every shot. I have a pre-shot routine, I'm gabbling less than usual, I'm pacing out distances. I munch on bananas, energy bars, apples and nuts while sipping water and sports drinks. All at the same time.

I even make sure I'm not sidetracked by Martin's usual antics. Simple strokeplay or straightforward Stableford never seems enough for him. He will insist on games within games, each with a more obscure set of rules than the last. I think he dreams them up as he goes along.

'Right,' he says, 'to spice things up, let's play Texas Scramble for the first three holes, then four-man Cha Cha Cha to the 12th, then alternate shot Bingo Bango Bongo. Off our Stableford handicaps, of course. Divided by 3.76. Depending on the wind direction. And let's end with a couple of holes of Dr Doolittle. And what about a fiver on nearest the pin at the 12th? And . . . '

I haven't got a clue what he's on about. I ignore him and write down my score.

I play neatly from the start and cause a bit of a stir with my drive at the 2nd hole, when I out-distance the rest by a good 50 yards. By then, however, Martin and Matthew are already exchanging words about banditry, while Roger has his own issues. He's too busy trying to locate the four-iron he's just flung into the undergrowth to spend much time on compliments. We all have our own concerns, once out on the course. As in life.

So nobody really notices that I'm three shots clear by the 9th – me, the one who always limps in last (apparently, I'm doing less well in the Bingo Bango Bongo, for some reason I never manage to fathom). Martin's the only real threat. Matthew, after his miraculous start, is now fulfilling his own prophecy and playing like a squash player and Roger's playing like a cricketer – some nice off-drives interspersed with the odd edge through the slips. As for me, I'm comfortably longer than Martin off the tee and I feel it's my game to lose rather than his to win.

I do my utmost to throw it all away on the 13th, when I momentarily forget how to play. Opting for a safe three-wood, I scuff the ball 60 yards along the ground, only to repeat the shot not once but twice on the way to a treble bogey. My chance of a single-figure round goes up in smoke there and then.

'Oops,' says Old Tom.

I seize up for the next few holes too, as I start to fret over the numbers, but I manage to get back into the groove just in time and finish on 13 over, two shots clear of Martin with the other two some way further back.

I've done it! I've beaten The Brothers! All of them! For the very first time! It's a great moment!

And nobody, absolutely nobody, notices. It's the concluding highlight of my year but nobody notices.

Matthew is still arguing his case ('Actually, 24 is quite reasonable when you consider . . . ') as we get back to the clubhouse, while Martin is consulting his BlackBerry calculator to try to decipher who won the Cha Cha Cha and Roger's wondering whether to go back for the three-iron he hurled into the River Mole on the way to the 18th green.

We toast Dad's celestial health, and Mum's health too. Matthew, Roger and I drink Guinness as quickly as possible while Martin tells us where he'll be holidaying for the next five years. It's a fine day but, like so many of my 'triumphs', it's not the one I'd envisaged. Not quite.

Driving back, Roger says that I should be proud of what I've achieved. And I am. But again, echoing my best previous rounds, it feels as if something's missing.

And I can't help thinking that beating my brothers did not much matter after all.

It feels as if I've missed the point.

NINETEEN

IT'S NEVER BEEN ABOUT THE FISH

'Golf is very much like a love affair, if you don't take it seriously, it's no fun, if you do, it breaks your heart. Don't break your heart, but flirt with the possibility'
— *Louise Suggs*

29 September – No days to go. Day 365. Basta. The End. Full Stop.

8 a.m. Emma tells us over breakfast that she no longer believes in the Tooth Fairy.

We must look disappointed because she quickly consoles us.

'But I do,' she stresses, 'believe in Father Christmas. And the Easter Bunny. And the Birthday Bunny.'

There's a pause. I can't help myself.

'I've never heard of the Birthday Bunny before.'

'Oh, I just invented him.'

The inside of my daughter's head remains a mystery to me.

11 a.m. I hadn't really planned any golf beyond The Brothers. That was meant to be that. But I find myself back at Poult Wood, on the final morning of my very last day.

I'm with Elaine. We used to work together at Reuters. She's not played for very long, but she's as keen as carving knives. She phoned up yesterday, on the off chance that I might want a game. I thought I was done but it suddenly seemed fitting that I should play out my year with a final fanfare.

Elaine is 2ft 6in tall, looks like Suzi Quatro and swings mainly with her arms – how she gets them around that considerable chest of hers I have no idea – while striking the ball 120-yard straight.

It's going to be a slow old round, I realise, but Elaine's seriously good fun. We'll have a good chat, I'll tell her about all the people I've met and the things I've learnt, and we'll conclude with beer and a discussion about the efficacy of sports bras.

Getting out of the car, I find I've left James's magic driver behind. I've accidentally brought the Precision one. The one that I hit as high as kneecaps. Damnation. I'll just have to try to do what Stacey told me. I'll exaggerate my lean to the right, rotate rather than sway and not rush back to the ball.

The 1st hole is a leisurely dogleg left. It's a three-wood or rescue. Unless you're foolhardy enough to believe you can produce a pinpoint draw around the trees with your driver. What the heck. I'm here for the craic. I set up, drop my right side, and hit the best drive of my life. Or, more exactly, a searing, screaming, foolhardy pinpoint 290-yard draw. It clips off a couple of leaves on the way round the corner and settles on the left fringe of the fairway, 60 yards from the green. I look at the club in bemusement. It's never done that before.

'Wow,' I say.

'Wow,' says Elaine.

'Wow,' says the man occupying a bench next to the tee box.

I par the 1st and the 2nd. On the 343-yard 3rd, though, we find our way blocked by a dawdler. He's on his own, an elderly duffer with time to burn and divots that fly twice as far as his ball.

We wait for three or four shots. Then we wait for three or

four more. We get bored. He's approaching the green at last. It must be safe by now, despite the wind behind. My honour. I take to the tee. I drop my right side.

'Fore!' Elaine and I both scream at the same time.

I've hit a huge, towering drive and it's heading the duffer's way. He ducks and the ball whistles past him. He looks back and gesticulates furiously. I look as apologetic as I can, considering how elated I feel. Elaine, giggling, takes a step back and points at me. I examine my club again. What the heck's going on? What sort of trouble are you getting me into here, Stinger? We reach my ball. We reckon it's gone 307 yards. The best drive of my life (again), and my first over 300. The duffer, scowling, lets us through.

And so the round continues. I've never, ever swung as freely. Most of the time, Elaine's asking for tips. Most of the time, I'm too speechless to reply. But whenever I hit the ball, it goes into orbit. I remember just two bad shots − a pulled nine-iron which needlessly buries into the face of a bunker and a dragged three-wood into the trees. Otherwise, I'm as inspired as I'm relaxed.

The best moment − inevitably − comes at the 16th. The 291-yard par four. The slight dogleg right. Mitch's hole. The one where I play a five-iron off the tee and he hammers his ball into the rhododendrons.

There's no way I'm playing an iron today. I tell Elaine what I intend: 'I'll cut my driver low around the corner and it'll run up just short of the green.'

Then I cut my driver low around the corner and it runs up just short of the green. The ball fizzes out low, with a deliciously delayed fade. It's the cleverest drive of my life. I chip on and birdie.

I end on 6 over par. Whatever the score says, I've never played better. I strike gloriously. I play unfettered. I fall in love with my 10-degree driver. Or rather, my swing at last does the club justice. And I realise that my round with Elaine is worth more than my 74, my 75s, my first round in single figures and The Brothers' Match all put together.

We drink beer on the balcony overlooking the final green and I end my year on the highest of highs.

I feel as if I've got the point at last. For the first time, I've let my game free. I've played for the pure fun of it.

And, driving home, the real secret of golf – or rather, the secret of my golf – finally comes to me.

I'm not playing low-scoring golf, not really. I just thought I was, for a while. But from now on I'm playing fun-filled golf. Life's too short, after all, to have a bad time on golf courses.

Or, put another way, the secret of golf, when all is said, is That Reason You Find, Be What It May, To Go Back Out And Play Your Next Round. Without that reason, golf would cease to exist.

And the reason I will go back out will be pure strikes. I will never play bad golf again, because golf will never make me feel bad.

My brother-in-law will shake his head when he reads this, but for me, John, it's never been about the fish.

TWENTY

POSTSCRIPT

It's 26 October, four weeks after the end of this book. Strictly, there's no reason for you to read this. But I can't resist the idea of coming full circle.

I'm in Florida, staying with Martin and his family at their holiday home.

Jan and Emma are in the pool. I'm on the golf course, playing with clubs borrowed from my sister-in-law. They feel as if they're made of over-cooked linguini.

Still. I'm on the 18th green, and facing a 6-footer, uphill and with right-to-left break. For the match. To beat my nephew, Andrew. You remember – that Andrew. Teeth-brace Andrew. Falsetto Andrew.

Martin is already out of the match but Andrew – no longer a chicken drumstick, more a seventeen-year-old, 6ft 2in rack of buffalo – has just parred the last four holes to draw level with me.

So I try to make myself, for once, take a putt seriously. I line it up.

'For the match,' I remind myself. 'Against Andrew. That Andrew.'

I make a couple of practice strokes. I address the ball. I breathe out. For the match. And then I hear Old Tom resorting to blackmail.

'If you don't make this putt, you're giving up the game – for good, this time,' he whispers.

And I start to laugh. I walk back from the putt and laugh.

Martin and Andrew probably saw no more than a fleeting smile. It felt as if I was laughing, but it turns out that it was internal.

Inside, I'm laughing to find myself back to my old tricks, listening to Old Tom and beating myself up for no good reason. I'm laughing at the idea that I might attach such importance to a putt. At the notion that putts can exorcise demons (or, at least, demonic nephews). At the very suggestion that I could ever again consider giving up this most marvellous of games.

And, with that, I banish Old Tom from my mind, I address the ball, barely pause, and I stroke it into the centre of the cup.